☑ W9-CCA-680

Stanley Collins

Courage And Submission

A Study Of Ruth & Esther

A BIBLE
COMMENTARY
FOR LAYMEN

A Division of G/L Publications
Glendale, California, U.S.A.

© Copyright 1975 by G/L Publications
All rights reserved
Printed in U.S.A.
Second Printing, 1976

Published by
Regal Books Division, G/L Publications

Glendale, California 91209, U.S.A.
Library of Congress Catalog Card No. 74-32323
ISBN 0-8307-0310-1

Contents

A Teaching Manual and Student Discussion Guide
for use with this book are available from your
church supplier.

Introduction

The similarity between the books of Esther and Ruth is too obvious to be missed. Both women were brought by God into unusual marriages: Esther, an Israelite, to a heathen king; Ruth, a Moabite, to the Israelite Boaz. Through these marriages God was to accomplish His eternal purposes.

Esther was the instrument God used to deliver His people from extinction in Persia. Ruth was to become the great-grandmother of David and thus an ancestress of our Lord and Saviour Jesus Christ.

Both books teach valuable lessons about God's dealing with His people. Ruth is a love story depicting, in the tenderest terms, Christ's role as kinsman-redeemer of mankind. Esther, in spite of the fact that the name of God is never mentioned in its pages, is an excellent illustration of His providence, His ability to overrule the most difficult situations in order to bring about His own plans.

Both books will speak to your heart if you will open it to God and to His message for you.

1
Ruth
1:1-22

Love Story

Ruth is a love story. It's all about love of various kinds. There's the love of a daughter-in-law, Ruth, for her mother-in-law, Naomi. There's the love of a man, Boaz, for a woman, Ruth. And overshadowing the whole lovely story is the love of God for His people. His love is displayed not only in His gracious provision of a home with Boaz for the two women, and of a wife's love and devotion for Boaz, but also in the divine descendant of that couple, the Lord Jesus Christ. He is the ultimate expression of the redeeming love of God. And the romance of Ruth and Boaz not only provides us with a story about some of our Lord's ancestors, it also provides us with a "type" or picture of the kinsman-redeemer provision which is one facet of what Christ did for us in His death and resurrection.

The historical setting of the book of Ruth is the era when the judges reigned in Israel. The people had been in the land for some time now. Joshua had brought the people over Jordan, had seen God's tre-

3

mendous work at Jericho, and eventually had sub-
dued the inhabitants of Canaan. The land had been
distributed among the various tribes and God had
given rest to His people. But after Joshua died, the
nation returned to its disobedience and evil ways.

The people had enjoyed government by one man
for long periods—first with Moses, then with Joshua
—and they seemed lost without such leadership.
They went downhill in every way. The terrible situation is summed up for us in Judges 17:6: "In those
days there was no king in Israel, but every man did
that which was right in his own eyes." Unbelievable
atrocities were perpetrated in those days. Some sec-
tions of the book of Judges contain accounts of such
cruelties that they are difficult to read in public worship.

Every year Israel sowed her seed and reaped the
harvest; then the Midianites would attack and take
away all their hard-earned produce. These were difficult days for Israel. As they suffered oppression by
their enemies and the resulting economic hardship,
they felt anything but "the chosen people." In fact,
this period of time proved to be one of the very lowest
and toughest in the whole history of the nation.

The book of Ruth contains no evidence concerning the human author, but tradition has always
named Samuel.

The importance of the book, examined in the light
of the genealogy of Christ (Matt. 1:5), is very great.
The book also foreshadows the future union of Jew
and Gentile in the Lord Jesus.

As a piece of literature it is a gem, a pastoral idyll
with a lovely romantic touch which makes it very
readable and enjoyable!

4

Basically it is a story of people and of the amazing sovereignty of God over their lives as He overrules their decisions (and their mistakes) to accomplish His will.

A famine is ravaging Israel, so Elimelech and Naomi decide to emigrate to Moab. Their two sons marry two girls in Moab. But tragedy strikes, and in a short period Naomi finds herself a widow and childless—her husband and her sons dead. In much bitterness she decides to return home and spend her seemingly miserable future there.

Ruth, her daughter-in-law, insists on coming with her. Once they have settled down in Bethlehem, Ruth, looking for work, picks the field belonging to Boaz, a wealthy relative of Naomi. Ruth and Boaz meet, fall in love, and marry. Their son becomes the light of Naomi's life and ultimately a man of great importance—Obed, the father of Jesse and grandfather of David!

There is no book in the Bible which shows more clearly the providence of God directing and controlling the apparently trivial incidents of daily life in order to bring blessing to many lives and lasting glory to the name of God.

Ruth is rich in "types" for the Christian believer. Much of the book can be understood on a spiritual level to give us vivid pictures of Christ's love for His bride, the church.

As we turn to study the book in detail, we must remember that faith was at a minimum among the people at this point in time. Consequently, obedience to God was almost unheard of. It was truly a dark passage of history.

The Decision to Emigrate/Ruth 1:1-5

The making of decisions is the making of character. Our choices will show what we are now, or they will determine what we will become; so major decisions must be made carefully. Our motives are important. Sometimes we are moved by the very natural instinct for self-preservation. This is often the reason for emigrating to another country.

It is a revolutionary experience to move all you have and to begin a new life in a country that has different customs, ideas and goals. You need to be very certain this is the right step before making it.

Millions found a home in the U.S.A. because life had become unbearable for them in their own lands. Millions of others came because they thought life would be easier here. They expected to find dollar bills dropping from the trees. They soon discovered it isn't quite that easy.

Make sure you carefully weigh all the alternatives before making big decisions, and always make room for the "unknown quantity." What looks so beautiful now can become a disaster within years!

Elimelech's decision to emigrate was made with Naomi's cooperation—in fact, from her statement in verses 20,21, she may have considered herself the prime mover in the decision—and was based purely on the economic situation. Living was tough enough under normal circumstances; with a famine to contend with, it seemed the sensible course to move out, to go where things would be easier.

God has often used famine to bring nations to a sense of need, and as a reminder to His own people that they should depend on Him. But instead of trusting God, Elimelech and Naomi decide to try to handle the situation their own way.

Their move to Moab might have looked wise economically, but it was a sad choice from the spiritual angle. It was almost like moving into the enemy's camp.

Moab and Ammon were a bad lot from the beginning. They were the results of incestuous relations between Lot and his daughters. (See Gen. 19:29-38.) Their descendants had always opposed Israel. They had refused them bread and water during their exodus from Egypt, and they had hired Balaam to curse the Israelites. Because of these deeds, God forbade the Ammonites and Moabites entry into the congregation of the Lord and told His people not to seek their peace or prosperity. (See Deut. 23:3-7.)

(Looking ahead, though, we can see how richly God's grace and mercy were bestowed on one individual Moabite named Ruth!)

In view of the facts about Moab, it hardly seems likely that Elimelech and Naomi consulted God in their decision to move to that land.

Nevertheless, the decision is made; the family moves to Moab. Apparently everything goes well at first, and the improved economic situation is much to their liking. The early years pass smoothly enough.

Then comes tragedy—one of those things which changes life completely, the "unknown quantity." Elimelech dies. Naomi has to face the devastation and desolation of bereavement. Everyone knows death is inevitable and unavoidable, but we never expect it to happen to us nor to our family. Now Naomi finds herself a widow. Only those who have traveled this road know the pain and anguish she suffers.

Naomi has her two sons, and they marry Moabite girls. It seems the two wives are fine girls who love Naomi and whom she loves. She sets about picking up the broken threads of life, and looks forward to enjoying the coming of grandchildren from her sons.

But tragedy strikes again, and a very savage blow it is, for Naomi's two sons die and she is absolutely bereft. After the shock of all these happenings she takes a long look at her situation and decides her best course is to return to Israel where she can pick up her life with former friends. She has nothing in Moab, except three graves, and so she announces her intention to her daughters-in-law, Ruth and Orpah. She has no hope in Moab, for there is no social security nor any kind of financial provision for her. As an added lure to return to Israel, she hears the news that the land is flourishing again. The famine has ended; a succession of good harvests has caused the news to spread far and wide, "The Lord had visited his people in giving them bread" (v. 6).

Naomi has no idea at this time how God is caring for her. In fact, she is sure He has forsaken her! How encouraging it is for us to know our heavenly Father watches over us. Even when we make our mistakes He can overrule them for our good.

Naomi's Farewell to Ruth and Orpah/ Ruth 1:6-14

Parting from loved ones is never easy. It is obvious there is a real bond of love between Naomi and her daughters-in-law. The three of them make their way to the border of Moab. It seems that the girls would continue with Naomi, but she feels such a thing would be useless.

Naomi exhibits a very giving spirit and demonstrates unselfish love in her deep concern for the girls' future. She thanks them both for being good wives to her sons, and prays that each might find another husband in Moab. Eastern courtesy demands that they again insist on coming with her, but Naomi points out they would have no hope of a marriage in Israel. What mother would allow her son to marry a Moabitess? Naomi says that if she had more sons she would be happy to give them in marriage, but this is impossible, so the girls must return home.

Verse 13 gives us insight into Naomi's mind, the turmoil she is suffering and her deep sense of responsibility for the situation her daughters-in-law were in. She states, "It is exceedingly bitter to me that you have suffered" (v. 13, *RSV*). None of us lives to himself. Our obedience to God will affect other people, as will our disobedience. One of the severest penalties for sin in this life is the sorrow and remorse you feel when you realize your sin has caused innocent people to suffer. We see this all around us when a man leaves his wife for another woman. He may feel that she asked for it and deserved it, and by this he tries to justify his action. But what of his children? They are innocent, but they suffer because of him, and so do parents and close relatives. People are either better or worse for meeting us. It is not that God waits to visit the sins of the fathers on the children (see Exod. 20:5), but some sins carry that awful possibility with them.

A child born of dissolute, drinking, immoral parents is going to suffer from birth, for some diseases are inherent. Sin pays wages right now. God will forgive your sin; God will remove the penalty; He will take away your guilt and the pain; but sometimes there are consequences in this life that cannot be avoided.

Naomi feels a sense of responsibility for the girls. She is not to blame for her sons' deaths, but maybe she is thinking, "If only we had stayed in Israel all this would never have happened."

Orpah finally bids her mother-in-law a touching and tearful farewell and makes ready to return home. But Ruth has other ideas.

Ruth's Amazing Decision/Ruth 1:14-18

"But Ruth clave unto her!" There is no parallel for this act of absolute self-sacrifice and devotion on the part of Ruth, not for the sake of husband or children but for her mother-in-law. Mothers-in-law have been the stock-in-trade for the comedian down through the centuries, but many of them have proved to be as devoted as any mother. This looks like that kind of relationship.

Naomi feels she cannot accept such a sacrifice, believing that Ruth can have no idea how terribly difficult life would be for a Moabite widow in Israel, so she urges her to return with Orpah and resume her former way of life. The question of nationality is both real and deep, but the greater problem is religion. There is no way Ruth could practice Moabitish religion in Israel, so Naomi feels she should accept the situation and return home.

There are many beautiful passages in literature where love is affirmed, but none can surpass the sheer beauty of Ruth's avowal of love to Naomi. It has become a classic, and many couples include her statement as an integral part of their wedding service.

"Intreat me not to leave thee, or to return from following after thee: for whither thou goest, I will go; and where thou lodgest, I will lodge; thy people shall be my people, and thy God my God" (v. 16).

This is a tremendous affirmation. Ruth has nothing to gain and everything to lose. She will be faced with a racial problem, and will find herself isolated and unwanted by the community. She is putting her life on the line. She is giving up her own nation and her rights as a citizen, and is moving into a strange country, one that has been the sworn enemy of her own for years.

Ruth knows that Naomi has nothing to offer her except poverty and hardship, but this she is prepared to accept. "Where you lodge, I lodge" has the ring of Christ's words, "The foxes have holes, and the birds of the air have nests; but the Son of Man hath not where to lay his head" (Matt. 8:20). Few, if any, would follow Christ on these terms, yet Ruth is prepared to go all the way with her mother-in-law.

"Your people, my people." Imagine giving up your people, your home, and your land to seek a new life in the land of your enemy, with no prospects and no promises, all because of your love and devotion to another person. This is the quality of Ruth's love for Naomi.

"Your God, my God." Even though Naomi is feeling very bitter about God's dealings with her, Ruth has evidently seen and heard enough over the years to know that Naomi's God was vastly superior to the deities of Moab.

Naomi sees that Ruth is "steadfastly minded."

This is no sudden decision made in a highly emotional farewell drama, but rather a calm, settled, deliberate and determined decision, possibly made some time before. Naomi sees that no argument will change Ruth's mind.

So, Naomi accepts the inevitable and the two journey on, until at last they come to Bethlehem, Naomi's home city from which she had emigrated years ago. Imagine her feelings! She had gone out with her husband and two sons to a life that promised so much; but now she has returned a widow with one daughter-in-law who is a Moabite.

The Bitterness of Naomi/Ruth 1:19-22

Naomi is welcomed by the community, which seemingly turned out in force to greet her. We can easily imagine the crowd's reaction in the one reported question, "Is this Naomi?" In this query we can read surprise and even consternation—"How she has changed," "She really has aged," "Moab has left its mark on her," "You can see she has suffered," "Losing her husband and two sons is terrible; you can see the effect it has had upon her." Naomi's reacton is swift, harsh, yet understandable. "Call me not Naomi (sweet or pleasant), call me Mara (bitter): for the Almighty hath dealt very bitterly with me" (v. 20).

Naomi recognizes that the happenings in her life were not chance misfortunes or disconnected events. She sees in them something of divine discipline and punishment.

She says, "I went out full" (v. 21). Now she recognizes that people are much more valuable than things, and that a family is one of God's richest blessings to humanity. Elimelech and Naomi left Israel for Moab

12

in order to improve their position—they were leaving famine for prosperity—but on her return Naomi knows how rich and blessed she was before she left.

Here is a lesson for us all. Treasure your family while you have them; it is fine if you can afford a beautiful house excellently decorated and furnished throughout, but a house is not a *home*. It takes people to make a home, and once the people have gone, furnishings and decorations are no compensation for their loss.

Naomi continues, "The Lord hath brought me home again empty" (v. 21). She is conscious that she is not in Bethlehem by accident, and that somehow her personal decision to return to Israel has been strongly influenced by God. "He has brought me . . ." indicates her conviction that He is still at work in her life even if it might mean further disaster. "Empty" is her word to describe her situation, not robbed by the Moabites nor economic conditions, but "the Lord hath testified against me" (v. 21). "This is His way of letting me know, and everyone else, that He is displeased with me for ever moving into Moab. Forget the Naomi you knew: sweet, pleasant, happy and tender. Think now of Mara: hard, cold and bitter because the Almighty has afflicted me."

Poor Naomi! Like so many of us, she is passing final judgment on herself and on the Lord before the Lord has finished! If only she knew how wonderfully and lovingly God is planning to make the remainder of her days happier than she can imagine!

All she can see is a grim future ahead, yet God is preparing the loveliest of all surprises for her. Her future is so good that Naomi would never believe it if He were to tell her.

13

Remember how Jacob reacted similarly when his sons said Benjamin had to go to the Controller of Egypt? He mourned and wept, crying, "Joseph is not . . . and ye will take Benjamin away: all these things are against me" (Gen. 42:36). Oh, that he might have known God was never working harder to bless Jacob than at that moment! God was arranging a great reunion for Jacob, Joseph and Benjamin; but all Jacob could see was immediate disaster. This is probably our biggest mistake today: we single out some experience, then judge God by this alone, wondering why He allowed it. So easily we forget His many blessings and daily benefits, the mercies which are renewed to us each morning.

The Sweet Trust of Ruth

While we can all sympathize with the distress of Naomi, it is now time to take a look at Ruth's great faith as she enters the Bethlehem community as a stranger and foreigner.

She too has lost much: her husband whom she obviously loved, and her home with him in Moab. Now voluntarily she had moved into this strange land with a simple faith that the Lord she is trusting will provide for her and protect her.

Let us try to imagine Ruth's position. Immediately after World War II in Europe there were strong hostile feelings between the British and Germans. They had tried to bomb each other into submission, which meant that for the first time the civilian populations were deeply involved in the agony, bloodshed, death and destruction of war. Soon British soldiers were returning with German brides. You can imagine the problem this presented to many British families, but think what it meant to the German bride! She was leaving her home, her family and her country to move into a new town on the island her own nation had been trying to destroy. Her difficulties and trials in those early days would be many. Only the strong, loving care of her husband would see her through.

This is Ruth's position. She is entering a country where there is real hatred of Moab, and she has no idea how she will be received. However, she has made her choice. She has the quiet confidence that since her life has been totally committed to God, He will not fail her, but will sustain her and fulfill His purpose in her life.

What a precious thing it is to have a faith like Ruth's! Trusting without worry. Resting and relaxing in His love rather than "sweating it out."

The closing verse in this chapter brings the first ray of light and hope to Naomi, "they came to Bethlehem in the beginning of barley harvest" (v. 22). What a wonderful time to come anywhere! Harvest time has to be one of the most beautiful occasions of the year. When Naomi last saw Bethlehem it was in a state of famine, so a bountiful harvest makes an amazing homecoming for her.

It is Ruth's first view of Bethlehem, and it must appear lovely to her as the crops wave in the gentle breeze, a field of ripe gold beneath a sky of azure blue. This view and the spirit of the season—joyful family get-togethers—must be filling Ruth with a sense of hope that this is a truly propitious start on her new life. If she is to seek acceptance in the new community she could choose no better time, for in their happiness at harvest the local inhabitants will be in a good mood to give Ruth a chance.

15

So we see the beginning of God's overruling in the lives of Naomi and Ruth. For different reasons, yet along the same path, He has moved them out of Moab and brought them into Bethlehem. It is here He needs them, it is here He will do that which He has planned so long . . . a plan that will someday involve David, Israel's greatest king, and beyond him our Lord Himself.

Let us always remember that God never makes a mistake. He knows what He is doing, but His thoughts are not our thoughts, and His ways are past finding out, for He knows the end from the beginning. When it might appear that God manipulates His people like pawns in a game of chess, always remember that the people most blessed ultimately are the very "pawns" He uses. We will see this clearly in the developments now befalling Naomi and Ruth.

2
Ruth 2:1-23

Ruth Goes to Work/Ruth 2:1-3

The opening statement of chapter 2 reveals something of Naomi's background. Elimelech had come from a wealthy family, and the family fortune had passed into the hands of Boaz, who by his ability and prudence had increased the fortune so that he could now be described as a "mighty man of wealth" (v. 1).

We'll never know Naomi's thoughts about seeking Boaz' help. Probably she felt, as "poor relatives" often do, that the wealthy side of the family is not too eager to acknowledge them!

Ruth now reveals another fine side to her character by taking the initiative and seeking work. She isn't looking for welfare, or saying "the world owes me a living," or depending upon Naomi to carry her through the rest of her days.

God has no time for idlers, and He never chooses His servants from loafers. A study of Scripture shows God picks His men while they are working—David in the sheepfold; Saul out looking for his father's asses; Amos plodding along behind the plow; Peter, James, John and Andrew mending their nets.

Far too many young Christian "drop-outs" from college sit around waiting for the Lord to lead them, failing to realize God is more likely to lead them when they are working for a living rather than idling their precious time away.

Ruth is not going to sit at home bemoaning her widowhood or wistfully dreaming of the past, or drifting into a fantasy of the future. She comes to Naomi with a clear-cut proposal: "Let me go out and find a job." Normally this could have been a major problem, but harvest time made it easier.

There was always work cleaning up the fields after the reapers. When the reapers reached the edge of the field they made a circular move, which left grain still standing in the corners. This was picked by the gleaners and became their own property under Israelite law (see Lev. 19:9,10 and Deut. 24:19). Many women gleaned in the fields and in this way obtained sufficient grain to carry them through the winter months. It was hard work, for in addition to the "corners," gleaners had the right to pick up all the loose sheaves except in the area where they were stacked ready to be taken to the barns. Every field was open to the gleaner. No union card necessary, no employment agency to be consulted, just choose your field, and get to work. This is precisely what Ruth does.

What happens next has to be one of the greatest examples of God's overruling providence in the Holy

18

Scriptures, and a lesson all of us need to learn in these days. Guidance from the Lord is promised to every believer, but it doesn't always come the way we expected it to. Never confuse feelings with leading. Don't expect a vision of angels to tell you what to do about each decision. If your heart is right, and you are walking with the Lord in the light of His Word, the ordinary decisions you make with your (hopefully!) sanctified common sense will prove to be the line of His leading.

Ruth goes out to work; no lights flashing, no band playing, no voice saying, "First lane on the right, second field on the left and enter by the red gate." Scripture says, "her hap was to light on a part of the field belonging unto Boaz" (v. 3). What to Ruth is just "blind chance" is ordered by the Lord. As surely as the star guided the wise men to Bethlehem, so the hand of the unseen God leads Ruth to that field.

Eliezer, steward of Abraham, said the same thing when he was seeking a bride for Isaac, "I being in the way, the Lord led me" (Gen. 24:27).

Can you remember some minor happening in your life, perhaps a chance meeting with someone that ultimately led to a life-changing experience for you? At the time you had no consciousness of God's leading, but now when you look back to that occasion you realize how wonderfully God planned it all.

Ruth has made her commitment to the Lord, and the Lord knows she means it, so she is under His loving care and protection. He will safeguard her, bless her life, and lead her along in the center of His perfect will.

How happy indeed are the people who leave their

choices with the Lord, for none live so easily, none live so pleasantly as those who live by faith.

Boaz Arrives and Meets Ruth/Ruth 2:4-17

Boaz does not visit his fields every day, for he has much business to keep him in the city. However, he comes this day. The reception given him by his workers makes us wonder, "How did relations between employer and employee get into the mess they are in today?"

Boaz' greeting and his workers' response is not perfunctory, but gives evidence of a real respect one for the other. They need each other. Boaz needs their labor or skill, and they need his capital. There is mutual respect and recognition of the other's rights, something sorely needed in our present society.

Boaz has many deputies, but he comes himself, moving through the fields and talking with his workers. Probably in his mind this is just another visit—nothing special—just checking that the harvest was going along well. Then suddenly it happens—he sees Ruth—and it is love at first sight even if he doesn't know it yet!

Immediately he asks, "Who is she?" There are many women gleaning in the field, but he only has eyes for one! "Who is this damsel?" he asks, like any man longing to know a beautiful girl. His servants quickly inform him, "She is the Moabitish damsel that came back with Naomi; she came this morning and we thought it would be all right to let her glean."

Can you see the scene God is preparing? Naomi, Ruth and Boaz. Ruth moves out and *by chance* selects one field; *by chance* Boaz comes down that one day and out of all the gleaners *by chance* he sees Ruth!

Now if you want to see a man's reaction when he really falls in love, watch Boaz. He goes to Ruth and says, "Don't work anywhere else; stay here with the other gleaners. There is plenty of work. And don't be afraid of the young men; they will not molest you in any way. I have given them their orders." (We can be certain such orders were very plain and unmistakable: "Do not touch!") "When you are thirsty," Boaz says, "don't wear yourself fetching water; just help yourself to that which the young men have drawn."

True love can always be seen in the protective care given by the lover. He becomes solicitous for the welfare of the one he adores. Boaz is eager to do everything possible for the young and beautiful Ruth, who replies to his great kindness by asking, "Why are you doing all this for me?"

Probably at this moment Boaz hardly knows what to say except to blurt out, "Because I have fallen head over heels in love with you." Instead, he manages to say that he has heard of her coming to Israel and of the great devotion to Naomi that caused her to make such a tremendous self-sacrifice. His appreciation of her conduct and behavior is obvious. He recognizes her not only as a girl of external beauty but as one whose nature more than matches her physical attractions.

Boaz' prayer for Ruth has almost the qualities of a benediction. It is a classic in its own right, and is one of the keys in the complete story of Ruth.

Boaz prays, "The Lord recompense thy work" (v. 12). When we remember what Ruth has done, we recognize that only God is capable of adequately rewarding such sacrifice. Who could determine a just salary for the decision Ruth made and the action she took?

"Under whose wings thou art come to trust" (v. 12). Ruth would discover daily that the greatest umbrella of security in the world is resting in the will of God. The description Boaz uses of God's guardian care—"under His wings"—reminds us of Christ weeping over Jerusalem and declaring, "How often would I have gathered thy children together, even as a hen gathereth her chickens under her wings, and ye would not!" (Matt. 23:37).

Ruth's response is very warm and friendly, and extremely courteous. She is conscious of being a "foreigner," and like most people prepared for the worst, is appreciative when she gets the best. Her words convey to us the grace and goodness of her heart; she had obviously had some concern as to how men might treat or ill-treat her in her new country. To be spoken to so kindly was a source of great comfort to her. When she says, "Thou has spoken friendly unto thine handmaid" (v. 13), she is saying "What you have said went right to my heart and has reassured me."

Boaz is still anxious to do all he can for Ruth. He has already told her to help herself to the water, and now he seeks to make every preparation for the meal break! Eating and drinking, he wants her with his group, and he makes every provision for her. "Dip thy morsel in the vinegar," he tells her. This is still a common custom in the East, as it was when our Lord was here on earth (see John 13:26). The vinegar was probably the sour wine commonly used. "And he reached her the parched corn" (v. 14). He certainly is not too far away from her! Parched corn is a favorite food in the agricultural communities of the East even today. The ears with the stalks attached are tied into small bunches. A fire is made from dry grass and thorn bushes, and the corn is held in the fire until the chaff is burnt. The roasted grain is then ready to be eaten.

Ruth completes her meal and takes her leave to return to her gleaning. Once again Boaz intervenes on her behalf, this time to ensure that she will have a very successful day in his field and will not think of moving to another area!

Gleaning among the sheaves was generally forbidden, but now the restriction is lifted for Ruth. Furthermore Boaz orders his servants to leave some sheaves lying around especially for her! It is amazing what men do when they really fall in love, and Boaz cannot do enough for the young Moabitess who has truly won his heart.

Ruth continues her work, not knowing special provision has been made for her. As the day is ending she gathers up the fruit of her toil and makes her way back to Naomi with whom she can share all the wonderful happenings of this quite amazing day.

The Homecoming of Naomi/Ruth 2:18-23

We can imagine the thoughts of Naomi this day. How would Ruth fare? Would she be accepted by the gleaners? How would the men treat her? A beautiful widow in a strange country is vulnerable indeed.

Eventually Naomi's thinking is ended as Ruth arrives with the result of her work—an ephah of barley. The daily portion of manna allotted to the Israelites in the wilderness was the tenth part of an ephah per person, so you can imagine the quantity of food that Ruth collected. If there had been an Olympic Games event for gleaning Ruth would have walked away with the gold, silver and bronze medals.

Naomi's delight is obvious as her questions come pouring out . . . "Where did you work? Whose field were you in? How did you gather so much?" She awaits Ruth's answers but she could never have expected such a revelation. Ruth said, "The man's name was Boaz and he was so kind, friendly, and tender, and he took such great care of me. He gave me water and had me share the meal with him."

As soon as Naomi hears the name of Boaz, her heart leaps, her faith revives, and for the very first time in the book she is praising God! "May he be blessed of the Lord who has not withdrawn his kindness to the living and to the dead" (v. 20, *NASB*). She then discloses that he is a near kinsman, in fact one who has the right to redeem.

This intriguing law of the redemption of a childless widow is set forth in Deuteronomy 25:5-10. (It is called the *levirate* law from the Latin word *levir*, "husband's brother.")

Under this law, the kinsman was to take the widow as his wife and to raise a son to keep alive the name of her deceased husband. (If the widow already had a son this did not apply.) There was nothing immoral in this arrangement. The kinsman was not taking a mistress nor choosing another woman. He had no choice in the matter (except to refuse his duty and accept the consequences as described in Deuteronomy). A widow might be young and attractive, or she might not appeal to the kinsman at all; but either way he had his duty to do as a kinsman and redeemer.

24

Ruth discloses that Boaz has asked her to stay on through the barley harvest and the succeeding wheat harvest as well. Naomi heartily agrees. Maybe she can see developments already—for onlookers generally see most of the game!

The days and weeks slip by and Ruth continues her gleaning in the fields of Boaz, happy in the knowledge that God is on the throne and that He who has provided so wonderfully through the gleaning will provide something else when the harvest is finished.

3
Ruth 3:1-18

Naomi Takes the Initiative/Ruth 3:1-9

One of the very beautiful things about Ruth is the way she shares everything with Naomi. She is not too old to ask advice and not too self-sufficient to act upon it. Many a mother can learn from Naomi to plan carefully for her daughter, teaching her to trust God for her life partner rather than "chasing everything in trousers." The best matchmaker is God! Who else could there be? He made man, then made Eve for him. He knows the requirements of every man and woman.

Marriage is the biggest decision we make outside salvation. If ever we need the guidance of God in our lives it is right here. God never makes a mistake (though we do) and the best marriages are still made in heaven!

26

Naomi is not trying to help God out, only moving along the road which He Himself has opened up. It is now time for the winnowing on the open threshing floor, and soon the area will be filled with workers, both men and women.

This was the time of the year when Midianites had made a habit of invading the land and taking the crops that had been threshed. So now the Israelites took the precaution of sleeping out in the threshing floor during the time of the winnowing. Some came with their families, the children helping to carry the wheat to the threshing floor. At a busy time there could be hundreds of people engaged in this operation and it was a family affair.

Naomi knows Boaz has no wife, and in this sense no one to care for him when he is sleeping out. She feels that since he has shown such care towards Ruth, he will welcome her presence. She knows he will not misunderstand the situation: Ruth will never be taken as a "camp follower" nor will Boaz take advantage of her.

Tonight's the night! Whatever Ruth wore to go gleaning, it will not do for tonight. This is Ruth's big moment; she is having the whole treatment and Boaz is to get the whole works! The right perfume . . . hair fixed in the most attractive manner . . . the most beautiful dress. Naomi gives one more word of fine advice to Ruth: "Wait till he has had his meal," for so often the way to a man's heart is through his stomach! Certainly the wrong time to seek favors from any man is when he is hungry. Wait until he has had a good enjoyable meal and your chances of success will increase about 100 percent!

One thing needs to be made very clear at this

27

point. Naomi is not suggesting that Ruth do anything improper. And knowing Ruth's close walk with God, we can be sure she would not contemplate any kind of behavior that would harm her relationship with Him.

The threshing floor is an open place, the people sleep under woolen blankets as a protection against the cold nights. Naomi tells Ruth to go where Boaz is, and when he is asleep, to lie down across his feet to give him added warmth. When he discovers she is there, she is to follow his instructions.

Ruth's obedience to her mother-in-law is quite re-markable, but we need to remember that she is among a strange people with customs unknown to her. So she is more than happy to follow Naomi's instructions.

It is one thing to promise obedience with words, but actions speak louder than words, as every mother knows. Ruth not only says, "All that you say to me I will do," but she carries it out to the very letter. She does not question Naomi on the possible outcome, nor quarrel with her suggestion. She trusts herself to the never-failing care of the Lord, and moves out to the threshing floor.

Boaz completes his evening meal, and now pre-pares to settle for the night. Secure in his blankets, tired from the exertions of the day, he is soon asleep. As soon as Ruth sees this, she moves in quietly, gen-tly uncovers his feet and lies down to bring added warmth and comfort to him.

At midnight Boaz is awake, thinking he hears something. Habit has made him and his companions light sleepers, ever ready for the slightest sound which might herald another marauding band from

Midian. When he turns over he becomes aware of a woman lying at his feet. There is no light he can switch on, no candle he can light, so he can only ask, "Who are you?" and wonder who will answer. He is certainly expecting the worst, and no doubt he is filled with trepidation and he waits for the answer to his question. How like all of us! We never expect the unexpected to be good! If we receive a telegram, we think it must be bad news!

What a wonderful surprise is awaiting Boaz. The one person he would long to see more than anyone else, and even in the dark more beautiful than he had seen her, with her gentle words, her smile and perfume working wonders! "I am Ruth thine handmaid," she says. Just a few simple words, yet coming from the lips of the one he loved, it gave Boaz unbelievable joy. She continues, "Spread therefore thy skirt over thine handmaid; for thou art a near kinsman" (v. 9). The custom was (and still is observed by the Jews) to cover the bride with a Talith, or fringed garment belonging to the bridegroom, in token of his authority over her and his obligation to protect her (see Ezek. 16:8). Boaz has the right to redeem, and Ruth is now asking for his protective care on a much more permanent basis.

The Loving Care and Provision of Boaz/ Ruth 3:10-18

Boaz' response is spontaneous and full of gratitude for Ruth's thoughtfulness and consideration. He is really overwhelmed by this touching demonstration of her concern for him. He reveals one line along which his thoughts have been traveling: the difference in age between himself and Ruth. He has been talking to himself, no doubt, remembering that he must not mistake kindness for love nor start thinking that he is to be the lifelong partner for the young and beautiful Ruth. It is almost with relief that he says, "Thou followedst not young men, whether poor or rich" (v. 10). He promises her his complete protection and assures her of his total respect for her position. At the same time he bears testimony to her character and declares that the whole city is fully aware that she is a virtuous woman—no easy thing for a beautiful young widow, and a foreigner.

What an excellent testimony to the quality of life exhibited by the young Moabitess since she crossed the border into Bethlehem! She has kept herself in such a manner that none has molested her in any way. She is a rare jewel; her qualities and convictions are sorely needed in present day society.

There is, however, a major problem to be faced by Boaz. There is a man who is a closer relative than Boaz. The Jewish law specifically required the next of kin in blood relationship to act the part of the kinsman. If this was impossible because of separation by distance, ill health, mental incapacity or financial inability to take on the responsibility, then the second in line could become the kinsman-redeemer. Boaz is second in line. Boaz vows before the Lord, even as he promises Ruth, that he will seek a settlement of the matter as speedily as possible. Then he urges her to rest comfortably until morning.

Taking over the duty of a kinsman was no light matter and not readily undertaken by anybody. Boaz is a bachelor, so he has no wife nor children of his own to be concerned about. And Ruth of course is a very attractive young widow. But a kinsman might have a wife and children of his own. Still, as kinsman-redeemer, he must take over all that was his brother's —land, houses, businesses, mortgages and debts. He was required to father a son and raise him so that his brother's name would not die. One can see the many advantages in such an arrangement. It saved the widow from becoming easy prey to "wolves" and tricksters. The kinsman assumed responsibility for her well-being.

Only the kinsman could redeem, and he could only redeem that which he assumed. This is a very important factor in the spiritual lessons from the book when we think later of our Kinsman-Redeemer, the Lord Jesus Christ.

Boaz is anxious to protect Ruth's good name and reputation, and so he urges her to return before the general activity of the day begins. Her visit to him at night could be misinterpreted, and he does not wish her to face any embarrassment.

He loads her with all the barley she can carry as a gift to Naomi. (This is known as "getting in good with the girl's mother"!) This gift would speak louder than words as a clear indication of his feelings towards Ruth. Naomi has traveled this road before, and she sees all the signs of true love . . . maybe she can smell orange blossoms and hear church bells, too!

Naomi's advice to Ruth in verse 18 is something we all need to heed carefully. "Sit still . . . until thou know how the matter will fall." This is extremely difficult to do at any time, but especially so when the deepest emotions and feelings of your heart are involved. "Sit still," for a higher hand than yours is leading, a vastly more loving heart than yours is caring, and He has a bigger purpose in our lives than we shall ever know. How much we lose in peace and blessing because of impatience and our unwillingness to wait.

How many lives have been messed up, homes broken and hearts shattered through this very eagerness to get married. Some mothers, who ought to know better, will push a daughter to the altar almost with the first fellow she dates. They seem to feel that if a young woman is not married by nineteen years of age she is "on the shelf" forever. Parents, don't rush things with your children. We make more mistakes through haste than through waiting. "Marry in haste, repent at leisure" is a sound adage, tragically illustrated only too often in our day and generation.

Ruth's rare qualities are seen again in her sweet obedience and the gracious way she waits in calm serenity. She knows that the Lord she covenanted with before leaving Moab is still caring for her. Her life is in His hands.

Naomi's closing statement is so true! "The man will not rest until he has settled it today" (v. 18, *NASB*). To Ruth, sitting at home waiting, it may seem the longest day she ever lived. But God is working. He is preparing a wonderful outcome far beyond the boundaries of human understanding.

4
Ruth 4:1-22

Boaz and the Kinsman/Ruth 4:1-6

Boaz now sets up, according to the prescribed law, a meeting with Naomi's next-of-kin so that the question of redemption can be settled once and for all.

The gate of the city was where the elders of the community met, discussed projects, put forward civic schemes. Here was the final authority for all civic matters. What was decided at the gates became law. The language of the day incorporated the word *gate* to embrace the thought of counsel, discussion and decision. People would say, "the gate decided this" or, "Let us ask the advice of the gate." It is in this connection that our Lord Jesus said, "I will build My church; and the gates of Hades shall not overpower it" (Matt. 16:18, *NASB*). (The plans, schemes, ideas and attacks of hell will all fall before Him!)

Boaz now has to wait until the kinsman arrives. He has planned his approach carefully, yet correctly. The next hour or so will settle it all. At last the kinsman appears. Boaz calls him over and invites him to sit down with him. An interesting word for *called* is used: it does not mean a gentle invitation, but something more like a "respectable bellow." He is taking no chance he will not be heard! This is a casual enough approach— and this mode of operation continues. Boaz is "playing it cool" in this early stage. "Do you remember Naomi who lived here years ago and emigrated to Moab with her husband and sons? Well, she is back again, a widow, and she wants to sell the piece of land that belonged to her husband, Elimelech, so I thought it my duty to let you know. I am perfectly willing to buy the land but as next-of-kin you have prior claim, so let me know your pleasure. If you wish to buy it, do so. If you decline I will purchase it and give Naomi the proceedings."

I wonder if the heart of Boaz ceased beating for a moment when the kinsman said, "Sure, I will redeem it." The answer was quick and determined, so now Boaz brings out the decisive factor. "It is an excellent buy and you have made an excellent decision. There is just one minor problem. The day you buy the land from the hand of Naomi as kinsman, you assume full responsibility in caring for her and also for Ruth the Moabitess, because she is the wife of the dead son. Of course you realize that as Ruth has no son, you will have to do the conjugal duty of husband in the hope that a son will be born to carry on his father's name." (Remember Deut. 25:5-10.)

The kinsman's enthusiasm dies. A good bargain is one thing, but additional responsibility is quite another. His new decision is just as quick and determined as his former one! "I cannot redeem it for myself, lest I jeopardize my own inheritance" (v. 6, *NASB*). Perhaps he has some economic problem, but the use of the words "jeopardize my own inheritance" must refer to the fact that Ruth is a Moabitess, a stranger from a despised people. It would be difficult enough to raise a child to his dead brother even if the wife was of pure Jewish stock. But to have a Moabitess in the family, and the possibility of fathering a Moabitish/ Jew, is unthinkable!

Another part of his reluctance may stem from the need to spend his own money on something that will eventually belong, not to him, but to Ruth's son. He is now so anxious to be rid of the whole responsibility that he turns to Boaz and almost begs him to "redeem my right to yourself."

Boaz can now rightfully, clearly and legally take over all that was Naomi's; but best of all, the way is wide open for him to claim the lovely Ruth as his bride. He may be thinking, "This is my lucky day," but over all the human decisions stands Almighty God. In His sovereign power He is overruling and working out His eternal purposes through human channels, even if those channels are not aware of His guidance in such vital decisions.

The Public Ceremony/Ruth 4:7-12

Boaz calls the civic leaders and the general public to witness the official transaction, the handing over of the kinsman's duties to him. It is a simple act, the removal of the shoe from the one to give to the other. In some cases under the law (see Deut. 25:8-10) this ceremony was anything but pleasant! When the kinsman refused to fulfill his obligation to his deceased brother, then the widow would remove his shoe in the presence of the public, spit in his face, and declare "Thus it is done to the man who does not build up his brother's house" (Deut. 25:10, *NASB*).

But there is no such shame nor indignity here, Boaz is thrilled to be in reach of his ultimate goal— Ruth! He calls upon the assembled group to witness that he now accepts the full responsibility of kinsman-redeemer to Naomi, and gladly declares that this includes the taking of Ruth to be his wife.

The Wedding of Ruth and Boaz/
Ruth 4:13-22

Amid all the good wishes surrounding the happy couple is one in the form of a benediction, which was prophetic to say the least, and had a truly amazing fulfillment! Here it is: "The Lord make the woman that is come into thine house like Rachel and like Leah, which two did build the house of Israel: and do thou worthily in Ephratah, and be famous in Bethlehem: and let thy house be like the house of Pharez, whom Tamar bare unto Judah, of the seed which the Lord shall give thee of this young woman" (vv. 11, 12). Keep in mind these words, *Ephratah*, *Bethlehem* and *Judah*, and see what happens!

Ruth and Boaz are married, and soon there is great joy at the news of an expected child. A son is born to the couple. Now Naomi comes back into the picture again, no longer bitter, but deeply thankful for the unfailing goodness of the Lord. She is reminded of this by the women who so rightly say, "This baby will restore your life (keep you alive), and be a nourisher of your old age" (keep you young). Everyone blessed with grandchildren of their own know the sweet and blessed truth of that.

Now follows what must be one of the most gracious tributes paid to anyone at any time. It is from women to a woman; it is from older women to a young woman, and that young woman a foreigner; and it is couched in terms of unmistakable admiration: "Your daughter-in-law, who loves you and is better to you than seven sons ... " (v. 15, *NASB*). This reflects the greatest credit upon Ruth's life since she entered Bethlehem.

Naomi cares for the young child, and Boaz and Ruth continue a normal family life in the agricultural community of Bethlehem. The infant is named Obed, which literally means *serving* or *worshiping*.

Ultimately, Obed reached manhood, married and had a son named Jesse, who in turn became the father of David, and it is with David that the brief historical record ends, along with the book of Ruth.

Let us now see how the "wishes" of the women at the wedding were fulfilled. For Ruth it was that she might become as great and well known as Leah and Rachel, the wives of Jacob and mothers of the twelve sons whose descendants became the twelve tribes of Israel. Ruth is the great-grandmother of David, God's choice to be king. Bethlehem became the city of David, beloved by him, his abode when all the battles and journeying were through.

But it was not to end there. Even Ephratah would become well-known as the area in which Bethlehem was located. Micah the prophet was to say of it hundreds of years later, "But thou, Bethlehem Ephratah, though thou be little among the thousands of Judah, yet out of thee shall he come forth unto me that is to be ruler in Israel; whose goings forth have been from of old, from everlasting" (Mic. 5:2). This wonderful Messianic promise received its fulfillment hundreds of years later when the angels announced to the shepherds on the Judean hills, "Fear not: for, behold, I bring you good tidings of great joy, which shall be to all people. For unto you is born this day in the city of David (Bethlehem) a Saviour, which is Christ the Lord" (Luke 2:10,11).

Here then is the perfect and complete fulfillment of the women's wish. Ruth was in the line from which our Lord Jesus Christ was born, and in Him all the nations of the world are blessed.

God has moved in power, and the wheel has gone full circle. Sorrow, tears, heartache, bereavement, joy, peace, contentment and marriage have all been in the divine economy, and many lessons have been learned by the participants in the divine plan.

We see much to emulate and much to avoid. The lessons of the book of Ruth are many and varied and our final lesson will be devoted to them.

The underlying truth of God's sovereignty is that He is always working even when to us nothing seems to be going right. Even as Shakespeare says in Hamlet, "The times are out of joint" (disjointed and dislocated); and yet, when we get to the end of the road and look back, we can say with Samuel Rutherford, "I will bless the Hand that guided. I bless the Heart that planned."

There did not seem much plan to it when Naomi suffered her three bereavements and her journey home could never be described as an act of faith, yet God was in her decision. It was God who put in Ruth's heart such a strong determination to return with Naomi, yet there is no suggestion that Ruth was conscious of it.

Let God have His way in your life; leave the choices to Him, believe He is always on the Throne, and remember He never makes a mistake.

5
Ruth 1-4

The Spiritual Lessons from Ruth

The book of Ruth is rich in its lessons for the Christian believer. Each of the major characters— Ruth, Boaz, and Naomi— has a specific message for us as we look upon them as representative types. Before we look at them individually, however, we should first take the overall message of the book, which is the sovereignty of God in the lives of the people.

Christians really need to have a sound scriptural view of God's sovereignty throughout all history and in this present time, for ignorance here will harm our whole concept of Him. Some have the idea that since He is almighty, all-knowing and all-seeing, we cannot tell Him anything; thus, they think, it is not much use asking for anything because He will fulfill His own will anyway. That is not the message of the Christian but the Muslim. We are not fatalists nor are we digits to be programed on a divine computer and punched out to form some unknowable design and purpose. God's ultimate purposes in the world will be fulfilled, of course, but He works with His people and for His people, silently planning for them in love.

Our basic problem is that we judge everything on the basis of how it turns out for us. If things go well we say how good He is; when they go wrong we ask, "Why me? Why did God allow this? Is He trying to punish me for something I did?"

A second common error is making our judgments before God has finished. Jacob is a perfect example with his complaint, "All these things are against me" when God was working overtime to bless him (see Gen. 42:36).

Having faith does not mean that we understand everything that happens. There are many things we do not and cannot understand, but by faith we are able to accept them. We do not become fatalists but rather active partners in God's program. We know God never makes a mistake. We see much we do not understand, but we know that He is in complete control of the situation. Though we are without answers to the problems, we rest in faith and trust, serene and calm, knowing that His perfect will shall be done.

Now let us look at our characters and the "type" that each one represents to us.

Naomi

She really is typical of many Christians of the type sometimes called "uncommitted" or "self-willed" or "carnal." There is no doubt that she believed in God and trusted Him in a general sense, but she was too taken up with the things of this world. She had her mind on earthly things, and this mind-set is revealed in her decisions and choices. It appears from her own statement that she was the driving force behind

Elimelech's decision to emigrate to the land of Moab. It was not a sinful decision, for she was not deliberately running into an evil situation, but it was selfish and unwise.

So many believers move away, leaving a fine church and Sunday School, and get into an area where there are very few spiritual opportunities but the pay check is $100 a month higher. How many lives have suffered spiritual loss through making such decisions! Of course, there's nothing wrong in getting a $100 raise, but to make that the only reason for uprooting a family and home is anything but wise.

Naomi obviously did not consult God over the decision, and in the first ten years when all was well there is no mention of the Lord! After three bereavements, Naomi is understandably broken. She blames God, saying, "The Almighty hath dealt very bitterly with me" (Ruth 1:20). The fact that God overruled all she did for His glory must never be taken as His approval of all that she did. Because it "all turns out well in the end" never means all that happened before the end was right!

Don't condemn Naomi, for you could be condemning yourself. Many of us are more like her than we are like Boaz or Ruth.

In spite of all she felt, she held on. When things began to move "her way" again she was quick to see the goodness of the Lord in the land of the living; and she changed her moans and complaints to thanksgiving and praise before she was through.

These are a few of the marks that indicate the Christian who has not totally committed all to Christ. His own will is dominant in his life rather than the will of God.

Ruth

Ruth represents the fully surrendered soul, the life that is handed over to the Lord Jesus without reservation. In the language of Frances Ridley Havergal's consecration hymn, "Take my life and let it be consecrated, Lord to Thee . . . take my hands . . . my feet . . . my lips . . . my love . . . Take myself and I will be ever, only, all for Thee."

Ruth came from outside, a stranger and an alien. She had no rights or privileges. She put her life on the line when she made her memorable vow to Naomi, the words of which we could well use as our vow to the Lord Jesus Christ. This was no pious statement used as the opening move in some religious game. She meant every word, and she gave momentum to her statement when she moved on in faith, crossing the border into Bethlehem.

Ruth's is the true life of faith and trust. Remember, she had gone through the desolation of bereavement and had the same grounds for complaint that Naomi voiced. Having made her choice, she followed on, believing God's way was the best way. She was obedient to the commands she received in the most difficult situations. She was exemplary in every action. Her mode of life won the admiration of those who could easily have become her enemies.

One of Ruth's greatest characteristics was her submission and her unruffled trust in the Lord. She stepped out in faith to glean, believing the Lord would direct her. She had no advance notice that she was about to meet her future husband (God is full of wonderful surprises). After all, who would expect to meet him gleaning barley?

If she had viewed things from a material angle she

would have probably stayed in Moab, where living would have been easier for her. God keeps His choicest blessings for those who trust Him implicitly, and Ruth was happy to leave her future in His hands. She did not know what tomorrow would hold for her, but she did not need to know, since she knew the One who held tomorrow in His hand was holding her hand and leading her along.

Her sole desire was to please God. No doubt, like any young widow, she hoped that perhaps in the future she might meet a suitable partner, but she was certainly not frustrated nor chasing after every male that appeared on her horizon. Can we really trust God to find us the right partner? This is a very tough situation for many singles of both sexes who hate the thought of being permanently single. But remember, you are a million times better off single and in the will of God, than married out of His will. Let God direct your steps in this vital area. He is never unmindful of us, and His bringing together of Ruth and Boaz is but an example of what He has done for thousands of couples since.

Ruth clearly pictures the believer who has found the true rest of faith in Christ and is discovering daily the greatness of His loving heart. May God give us both the desire and grace to live in our day as Ruth did in hers.

Boaz

He speaks to us plainly as a "type" of our Lord Jesus Christ, especially when we think of ourselves as the church, the bride of Christ.

Boaz came down to where Ruth was. He loved her just as she was, saw her need and her problems, and sought to change her life by becoming her kinsman-redeemer. Becoming her husband, he lifted her to his high estate, made her partaker of his name, and altered her status from the alien to the accepted and beloved. No price was too great for him to pay, no task was too great or too small, because of his love for her. He paid the full price in order to remove the barrier of the next of kin, and with great pride and joy let it be known to all that Ruth was now his bride.

Now let us see how beautifully this portrays the wonderful love of Christ for the sinner. First, He must come where we are. This involves the most glorious happening in all history, the incarnation of Christ. He was conceived by the Holy Spirit, born of the Virgin Mary, raised in Nazareth and Galilee. He passed through every stage of physical development —baby, toddler, infant, boy, youth, teen-ager, man— so that at the right time He could redeem humanity.

The very law of kinsman-redeemer is rich in teaching, for the kinsman could only redeem that which he assumed; so Christ could never redeem us unless He was our kinsman and assumed the full responsibility for us. How wonderfully He has done this, living, dying, rising again and continuing His life that we might be His own now and through eternity. He took our sins and our guilt upon Himself, and paid the full price on the tree, the "just for the unjust, that he might bring us to God . . . " (1 Pet. 3:18). Just as Ruth's status was changed so is ours; our new position brings us innumerable possessions and blessing. The bridegroom is able to express His abiding love in a million ways. In fact, Paul, writing to the Ephesians, states one reason for eternity is, "That in the ages to come he might shew the exceeding riches of his grace

44

in his kindness toward us through Christ Jesus" (Eph. 2:7). Christ's love is an unchanging love, and the covenant He established is unbreakable and eternal, sealed with the price of His own blood. Never forget for a moment that Christ gave His all for you.

Sometimes we describe our Lord as "altogether lovely." When we break down that word we see His unsurpassed love for His bride, the church! Christ gave His "all-to-get-her-love (ly)"; nothing in the universe is more precious to Him than His bride.

In heaven He is preparing the new home where He will welcome her and she will abide forever, enjoying the reflected glory of His presence and all that His wonderful heart has prepared for her homecoming.

How wonderful it is to behold God's love and grace in the Scriptures. Surely these four short chapters reveal so much to us that our lives must be greatly enriched as we read, trust and obey.

Faith comes by hearing and hearing by the Word of God, and the book of Ruth will certainly stimulate and strengthen the faith of all who read it. Remember, the God and Father of Ruth, Boaz and Naomi is also the God and Father of our Lord Jesus Christ, and through our Kinsman-Redeemer has become our God as well.

Let us walk daily with Him exhibiting humility and obedience like the traits which so beautifully characterized the life of the stranger from Moab, who became blessed by God, and was in the direct line of David and Christ.

God's way is always best; take it and enjoy the blessings of His Presence as you walk life's path until the day dawns and shadows flee away and you see Him face to face.

6
Esther
1:1-22

The Story of a Queen

The book of Esther comes in order of time between the sixth and seventh chapters of Ezra; together with that book and Nehemiah, its contemporary, it gives us something of the history of the people who stayed behind in Persia after the captivity ended.

Persia's king was Ahasuerus, identified more readily by his Greek name, Xerxes. He reigned from 485 to 465 B.C.

Of the human writer of Esther nothing is known. Some think Mordecai wrote it (basing their reasoning on 9:20-32), yet he would hardly praise himself (10:3). The vividness of the narrative and the accurate, detailed descriptions of the events point to an eyewitness account. The book was almost certainly written in Persia and is remarkable for what it does not contain: no reference to Jerusalem; no mention of the Temple; no word of the priesthood and the sacrificial system; and most amazing of all—no mention of the Lord God by name!

Because of these omissions some have questioned

the right of Esther to be included in the canon of Holy Scripture, but what *is* included in the book makes it impossible to doubt either its veracity or its authority. While it is true the *name* of God is not found in the Greek and English translations, yet the *hand* of God is seen protecting His people throughout the book. In the Hebrew text we find the name of God in the form of an acrostic several times; some have thought it was deliberately hidden in this way.

The object of the book is to give us a historical record of the wonderful deliverance of God's people from their total extermination as planned by Haman. There is no attempt to gloss over nor to remove the unpleasant things that took place.

The spiritual value of the book is limitless! The sovereignty of God in the affairs of a non-cooperating nation is never seen more clearly than here.

To the orthodox Jewish adult, it is one of the two books on which he gives his solemn oath. The first is obvious: the writings of Moses. But the second might easily have been the Psalms of David. Instead, it is to the book of Esther that he turns. Why? The answer is clear. Moses speaks of national deliverance from the Egyptians via the Red Sea; Esther speaks of national deliverance from Persia through God's two servants, Esther and Mordecai.

The Feast of Ahasuerus/Esther 1:1-7

Ahasuerus, as described by Greek historians, is a reckless, sensual, cruel and capricious man; this is certainly in line with what we read of him in Esther. The Persian empire dominated the world scene at the time. Territorially it extended beyond anything then known, from India to Ethiopia, covering 127 provinces. By any standard this was large. Ultimately it became the Greek empire, which later expanded. The final take-over was by Rome.

The area covered by the Persian empire included Egypt and extended through much of what is now North Africa, embracing people of many nations, colors and languages.

The emperor decided to put on an Empire Exhibition, a sort of World's Fair or "Expo 482 B.C." He made tremendous preparations for all his subjects who were able to attend. The whole celebration was to last six months. The program was wide and varied, catering to every type of taste.

One of the outstanding events of this memorable period was the great banquet given for all the visiting princes and dignitaries. All the glories of Persia were on open display: the riches of the kingdom, everything to delight the eye and much to incite envy and jealousy. Nothing was left to the imagination. Such beauty and splendor had never been seen before.

The color scheme portrayed in verses 6 and 7 would delight the eye and heart of any modern interior decorator. A galaxy of color filled the scene in excellent taste—green, white, blue, with cords of fine linen fastened to silver rings attached to marble pillars. Beds were of gold and silver against a background of red, white, blue and black marble. Even the gold cups from which they drank were different from each other in shape and in size. This was wealth! This was abundant extravagance deluxe!

The King and the Drinking of Wine/ Esther 1:8

Despite the fact that this would become a drunken

orgy and many foolish things would be said and done, there is a factor which many Christians would do well to note and learn. Although Persia made no claim to be a follower of Jehovah, and the present king was anything but a model of moral rectitude, still nobody had to drink wine unless he wished! If you wanted to drink yourself into a drunken stupor that was your right; but if you did not wish to partake of wine there was no compulsion. Neither king nor society required this of you for you to be "sociable."

So many Christians openly say, "I never drink . . . only socially," which, if you think it through, might become a theme for a TV comedy series! Whenever we want to justify our behavior to others—generally because of a guilt complex—we try to qualify the noun with an adjective: *social* drinking! What is the difference? You have to bend your elbow and swallow the drink for it to enter your body. If you believe it to be a wrong thing to do, then don't try to justify it by "being friendly." So many compromise their whole Christian testimony with those they are trying to win. An ever-present example of this is the "hail fellow, well met" drinking Army chaplain trying to be "one of the boys." The "boys" grow to despise him and in the hour of their deepest need he has nothing to offer them.

You are not less of a man or woman because you refuse to take liquor. It is a pity this one rule of the bygone Persian court is not in vogue in our present day society.

The Queen's Outstanding Decision/ Esther 1:9-12

The tragic figure of this banquet is Vashti. We

know little of her historically except that she was very beautiful, and as Persian women are among the most beautiful in the world, we can imagine what a delight to the eyes Vashti would be.

There were of course no rights for women in that day, not even for a queen. Women were totally subject to men, doing all the manual labor; when they married, they generally bore large families and spent the rest of their lives raising them.

Vashti, therefore, was very fortunate. She was wealthy and comfortable; she had plenty of servants and was the undisputed leader of feminine society in Persia, the empire's first lady.

She was having a banquet for the wives of the foreign dignitaries. Seemingly all was going well, with no hint of how these wonderful days would end.

Alcohol always exacts its toll as surely as sin pays its wages. After seven days of feasting and drinking, when the king's heart was "merry with wine" (v. 10), we see the way it affected him.

The king ordered his chamberlains to go and bring Queen Vashti so that she might display her beauty to his male guests. The main topic among men is generally women, and when the discussion is accompanied by drinking ... as the drinks are lowered so is the level of conversation. Ahasuerus was a sensual man. Alcohol may stir sexual passion, but can never satisfy it, so the king sent for his beautiful queen, so that she might display herself.

While it is true no man saw the face of a woman in public, and certainly no ordinary person had seen the queen's face, to think this was the extent of the king's desire is naive, and is to miss the point of what happened. Ahasuerus wanted his queen to display herself *totally* to his guests.

In a decadent day such as ours, when nudity is an everyday occurrence and some people seem to enjoy displaying themselves, we may think it strange that the king's command caused such a fierce reaction on the part of Vashti. She had everything to gain materially by coming, plus the approval of the king and praise of the spectators. To refuse would mean banishment and maybe death.

It would have been easy, perhaps, to do this thing and thus to please everybody. But Vashti showed herself to be a woman of character and determination. She was about to strike a blow for purity, righteousness and freedom, cost what it may. Her decision was made, it was announced and she would stand by it no matter what it cost. Just what it was about to cost her we shall now see in the next verse of Scripture.

The Royal Council's Recommendation and the King's Action/Esther 1:13-22

Vashti's refusal to obey the king threw the whole court into an uproar, for the Persian regime was based upon law and order. Even the king was personally subject to the laws he signed.

The word of the king was all-powerful. Therefore Vashti was starting insurrection and maybe even revolution. There could be no cover-up of such amazing news, with all the dignitaries from the overseas provinces flooding the capital. Court gossip is always a delectable item for any form of mass media communication, and this rebellion of the queen would be "hot line" news.

The Council acted quickly and decisively in the only way they could see open to them: they asked the king to depose the queen immediately, and to remove from her all her royal estate. This was to be followed by a decree that she should no longer come into the king's presence; she was to be cut off forever.

The king rejoiced at the recommendation and quickly gave his assent to the publication of the decree throughout the empire. This quick action would save the king's face and prove the widely accepted idea that a man must be master in his own home.

Natually the counselors were not thinking only of the king and empire, but of their own personal situations at home. If the queen could defy the king and get away with it, no man would ever feel safe again!

To us with our Western way of life and women's rights, it may seem, as Shakespeare said, "Much ado about nothing." But in Ahasuerus' realm, the total system of law and order required the subjection of women. Let us remember that Persia today and many Eastern countries that have not been subject to the gospel, still keep their women in what is bondage to Western eyes. The man is very much lord and master, the wife an obedient servant. She has no rights as a human being. Any benefits she may derive in life come from the success of her husband, not her personal efforts. No one has done as much to raise women to their proper state as the Prince of Glory, our Lord Jesus Christ.

Vashti was removed. The decree was accepted, and written into it the unmistakable command " . . . that every man should bear rule in his own house, and that it should be published according to the language of every people" [in the Empire] (v. 22).

7

Esther 2:1-20

**The Selection of a New Queen/
Esther 2:1-4**

So a queen had to be found. The king was a sensual man and would find sexual satisfaction with other women, but a queen was vital and must be carefully chosen.

You may recall several years ago the Shah of Persia was married to a beautiful queen; from all we could gather they deeply loved each other. But they discovered to their deep sorrow that they could not have children. The sad outcome was the abdication of the queen and the re-marriage of the Shah to another who did bear him a son to carry on the dynasty. This illustrates in some way how people would have no problem concerning Vashti's overthrow and the seeking of a new bride.

The choice of a bride to be queen cannot be done

hastily; it would take weeks and even months for some provinces to learn of the open competition. All the participants were to be "fair" [in the sense of beautiful], "young virgins." It would seem that it was a sort of Miss America contest. The girls who won at the local level moved to the county level, then to the state level and finally the state queens met in a central place for final selection.

The aim was to select the "most beautiful girl in the world" to be the queen. After all the eliminating contests the king would be his own judge in the grand finale!

The Arrival of Mordecai on the Scene/ Esther 2:5-7

We now have a little cameo picture of Mordecai the Jew. Notice throughout this book how those words "the Jew" stand out. From what happens eventually we know that such words were not a term of endearment but rather of derision and scorn. Mordecai had royal connections himself, in that, Saul, first king of Israel, was the son of Kish the Benjamite and Mordecai was also descended from Kish.

Mordecai was one of the Jews carried into captivity in the days of Nebuchadnezzar. Others who are now known to us were Ezra, Nehemiah, Ezekiel, Daniel, Shadrach, Meshach and Abednego.

After Cyrus, king of Persia, allowed Nehemiah to return and rebuild the walls of Jerusalem, the people of Israel eventually returned to their own land on a voluntary basis. But Mordecai, among others, elected to stay. We have no idea *what* influenced his decision, but in the light of future events we know *who* did— the Lord!

Sometimes on reflection, important decisions we have made turned out to be puffs of wind, while some of the more unthinking, inconsequential decisions in life have proved to be earth shattering. William Cowper, the English hymnwriter, puts this so perfectly in telling of a time when he was restrained from carrying out a terrible plan by a sudden, unpredictable and most violent storm.

"God moves in a mysterious way
His wonders to perform;
He plants His footsteps in the sea
And rides upon the storm.
Ye fearful saints, fresh courage take;
The clouds ye so much dread
Are big with mercy, and shall break
In blessings on your head."

Try to imagine Mordecai the day his homeland was invaded. Where will it all end? How will it end? Where is the Lord? Has He forgotten His chosen? Doesn't He care anymore? Have we been cast off? Why? Why? Why?

Private family sorrow was his portion as well. Loved ones were taken and he found himself responsible for a little girl—he a bachelor and a refugee. The plight of refugees has been before us since World War II—bombed, shelled, driven from home by invading forces—and we can imagine the concern and burden of Mordecai as he journeyed along the road to captivity. The first mention we have of the young girl states that she was "fair and beautiful." It is with these two people that God will deliver His own from total annihilation and extermination.

Esther is put forward as a candidate to be queen. This decision seems completely out of line with all that Mordecai had been taught concerning mixed marriages. Furthermore, while being queen of Persia was the highest position for any woman, yet to be the wife of a probably much older man, a hard-drinking sensual lout, was no nice thing for a lovely young girl to be involved in.

But with the hindsight we now have of Mordecai's faithfulness to God, matched by his obedience, we must feel that Mordecai felt that somehow, somewhere, God was going to take over this situation and use it for His glory.

The ability of God to intervene in the planned evil activity of man and to turn the whole situation to good eternal purposes is part of what we mean by the *sovereignty of God*.

The Selection of Esther As Queen/
Esther 2:8-20

A second area within the sovereignty of God is God-given favor with non-believing people. It is marvelous how God has caused His servants to get on so well in the most difficult situations, brought them out of seemingly hopeless conditions, and raised them to the highest power so that they became ultimately those channels through which He brought about His perfect will.

Joseph is an outstanding illustration of this truth. Disliked intensely by his brothers, he escaped death at their hands twice and was then sold as a slave into Egypt. "That's the end of him and his dreams" was their verdict as they made the homeward trip to Jacob.

In Egypt, Joseph might have been sold to anyone to be used and abused in many ways, but it was to

Potiphar's house he went. This man was captain of the guard to Pharaoh. The Bible states that God gave Joseph favor with his master. Promotion came fast as Joseph's abilities were recognized, and it seemed that all was working out well.

Then came one of those tragedies which cause His servants to say "Why, Lord?" Wrongly accused of attempted rape, circumstantial evidence against him, no one to plead his cause, he lost everything and was banished to jail. Only God knew Joseph was innocent, but He did nothing to save him, because God had bigger things at stake just then. The vindication of Joseph would be wonderful when it came in good time.

Pharaoh's butler and baker share their problems with Joseph, and Joseph is right in each case. When Pharaoh's wise men have no answer for their master's dreams, Joseph is sent for. God gives him favor with all, and he is made minister of Economics. Ultimately he rules the empire for Pharaoh. All this happened because God was working out His eternal purpose for His people. Joseph's verdict on God's leading, overruling and blessing is a classic, recorded in the statement he made to his brothers: " ... ye thought [planned] evil against me; but God meant [planned] it unto good" (Gen. 50:19-21).

Just as Joseph was the divine instrument in his day, Esther was to be in hers, and the days of preparation were important.

The chosen beauties, from overseas arrived and the stage was being set for the great day when the king would make his selection and announce to his people his new bride and queen.

One can imagine the feverish activities behind the

scene, probably many families offered generous bribes for special favors to their daughter. Yet of all the candidates in the custody of the chamberlain it was Esther whom he helped the most. His preference was seen as he gave her the best, yet Esther made no effort to win favor!

"Esther did not make known her people or her kindred, for Mordecai had instructed her that she should not make them known" (v. 10, *NASB*). This verse always impresses me with the thought that Mordecai had some consciousness that God was going to use this unusual situation and expand it for His own glory. It gives me an answer to the question of why Mordecai would allow his beautiful Jewish ward to run the risk of ending up married to such an unworthy character as Xerxes.

Mordecai also stayed very close to the scene. Verse 11 shows real concern, possibly agitation, as he goes back and forth, trying to pick up some vital information on how the young Esther was faring in such a strange country and even stranger surroundings. Undoubtedly she had lived a very sheltered life, but now she was on her own and placed in a very tough situation.

At last Esther's waiting was over. She completed the twelve-month preparation. She was soon to see the king, and even more important, he was to see her! This is a highlight in Esther's life, an amazing day, homecoming queen on a national basis!

Esther lacked nothing, for each girl had access to every beauty preparation available, and she could choose whatever clothes and accessories she wished.

I am sure most women could have managed this day successfully. Imagine your husband letting you loose in the best store in town and saying, "The lot ... whatever you want, just buy it and all that goes with it. I want you looking your best tonight." His checkbook would be hurting for the next ten years.

Queen for a day! This is Esther, but she had the one thing that is superior to every beauty aid—great natural beauty! Most of us, men and women, need all the help we can get. But whatever we get, however fine the improvement, it can never compare nor compete with natural young beauty.

Esther was not the first candidate the king had seen. Many may have stirred him, some he may have lusted over and desired with great passion, yet it is an amazing thing that when Esther is brought in it says, "the king *loved* Esther above all the women" (v. 17).

This word *love* is suffering greatly in this morally decadent age, but thank God there are many young couples who "fall in love." It certainly happened to the king, as his consequent behavior shows. He was a womanizer; he knew all the ropes, had all the answers, lived a life we would call dissolute. Yet now he was falling in love (maybe for the very first time) with a young, beautiful, pure girl.

He made his choice, announced his verdict: Esther was the new queen! Her nationality was not disclosed, nor required to be. The Persian empire embraced many nations and at least three colors—black from Ethiopia and North Africa, dark brown from India, and the lighter tan from the Mid-East. No problem yet about being a Jewess; yet again Mordecai said, "Keep quiet about it just now; I will let you know the right time to disclose your people."

Let us remember God had not taken Mordecai into His confidence and said, "In four or five years I have big plans coming up, so stay close and trust me completely." Mordecai was just walking with God, believing that at some time, some place, God would reveal His purpose, step by step. This was a test of faith, but he was going through strongly with the awareness that he had put everything on the line. Perhaps he had influenced Esther into something both he and she would regret all their days; still, all was in God's hands, and Mordecai rested right there.

8

Esther 2:21-23; 3:1-15

**The Plot to Assassinate the King/
Esther 2:21-23**

From the excitement, pageantry and rejoicing over the crowning of Queen Esther, our story now makes a dramatic change. A new figure is to dominate the scene; he is to give his name to history though not in the manner he intended.

From our perspective on history, we can see how wonderfully God was planning to use two people to fulfill His will, even though the total political and militaristic power of Persia would be arrayed against the seemingly inadequate forces of the Lord.

But let us see, now that God had placed Esther in a high position in Persia, how He used events to bring Mordecai into the king's favor.

Mordecai overheard a plot to assassinate the king. This was not a wild scheme with no chance of success, but a carefully prepared conspiracy by two men who were in the very place where they could murder

61

the monarch. They guarded the entrance to the king's presence and could enter at any time. All they had to do was choose the most appropriate moment for the assassination.

Ordinarily there would have been no way for Mordecai to get a message to the king. But now with Esther as queen, he was able to reach her immediately, and she in turn, told the king, who instantly started an official inquiry.

We live in a day when it takes ages to bring men to trial for deeds of which they are plainly guilty, and we are rightly concerned to give the accused every opportunity to defend himself. But we have some attorneys who are much more concerned with getting their clients free than with the establishment of truth and justice. The public too, must bear its full share of responsibility. Many of us think we are being "soft hearted" when we excuse evil and allow criminals to get away free because we do not wish to be involved. It is not a "soft heart" we have, but a "soft head"!

Justice moved more quickly in Ahasuerus' realm. Guilt was quickly established in the case of the would-be assassins. The sentence was announced and quickly carried out. Notice the closing sentence of the chapter " . . . it was written in the book of the chronicles before the king" (v. 23), this record was to play an unbelievably important part in the days that lay ahead.

The Unique Promotion of Haman/ Esther 3:1

We are surprised over and over again at the amazing material prosperity and temporal power of wicked men throughout history. From age to age, in all nations and communities, it seems that good people are kept down, while the wicked quickly rise to great eminence. Haman was a prime example of this fact. After a series of promotions he was ultimately placed in the highest place of authority and control, second only to the monarch.

A word about Haman's ancestors is appropriate. He was a descendant of Hammedatha the Agagite. You may recall that all Agagites and Amalekites should have been put away in Saul's day. (See 1 Sam. 15:1-9.) They were not, and now we are to see one of the results of refusing to carry out God's decree because they did not agree with it.

The Pride of Haman/Esther 3:2-6

The fact that people bowed down to Haman need not disconcert us, for the practice was customary with dignitaries among Eastern peoples. It still is today in most lands where the Islam faith is practiced. To a man like Haman, such reverence from the community was his life blood. He reveled in the obeisance of the people; it satisfied his ego and gave him the prominence throughout the kingdom that he so greatly desired.

Yet there was just one fly in the ointment . . . one black cloud in an otherwise perfectly blue heaven . . . one man, who refused to bow. He seemed particularly tall as he stood as upright as any man could. Friends of Mordecai urged him to cooperate. There was nothing to gain by holding out, they told him, and everything to lose. To Mordecai the reverse was true. As a Jew he could never bow to anyone except Jehovah.

There is always a time when we must stand and be counted. Have you noticed in Scripture how many of

God's servants withstood the power of kings and rulers in spite of the terrible threats made against them? They did not call committee meetings to decide the best course to take. This kind of decision is always made years before it is necessary. The very day your life is given to God, that decision is made for you. Before men you stand, shoulders back, head up; before God and God alone you bow in submission.

Just after the "miracle of Dunkirk" in World War II we in Britain waited daily for the expected Nazi invasions against which, humanly speaking, we had no chance. In those dark yet amazing days, a cartoon appeared in a national daily newspaper depicting a British soldier kneeling in prayer; above this simple picture were written the words, "We kneel only to Thee." The concept fired hearts and imaginations. The cartoon was reproduced in picture form and sold by the millions. You could see it in almost every British home.

Always remember there is a time to stand on your feet; make certain you are not kneeling nor running away on that day. Be a Mordecai!

Haman's reaction was violent. He was full of wrath; his anger against Mordecai was intense to the highest degree. It would have been easy to put Mordecai away, but how could the great and mighty Haman soil his hands with one solitary Jew? He would need to think of something better, more consistent with his greatness. Eventually such a plan came to his mind. "Why not exterminate the whole Jewish race?" The more his mind ran over this the happier he became. Eventually he decided he would plan and organize the massacre of Mordecai's people. It would require a new law signed by the king, but he knew that the right approach at the right time would take care of that, especially if, with the request, he would make a large donation to the royal treasury.

Haman Gets the King's Approval/
Esther 3:7-15

Haman's plan was set before the king. Like all such plans, it was full of lies. Like all anti-Semitic tyrants, Haman ignored the truth, being blinded by his consuming passion to destroy the Jews.

Haman was even prepared to finance the operation, knowing he would gain ample profit once he confiscated the property and treasures of those he had massacred. Ten thousand talents of silver was his estimate of the cost. So that we may understand the magnitude of the operation, in present day terms that is a sum close to $20 million.

A decree was drawn up, approved by the king, and duly signed and sealed. Then it had to be copied into the many languages used in the empire, and sent out to every place in the dominion. Haman's plan was evil and wicked beyond degree; a date was fixed for the universal annihilation of the Jews.

To avoid getting confused with the Persian calendar, we are simply switching the dates to our calendar to make it simpler. The edict was issued, say, on the first of January; D day (destruction of the Jews) was fixed for the 13th of December. No one was to escape. Old people, young marrieds, teen-agers and even babies would die. It was absolute and total extermination. It was nothing less than mass slaughter, totally unjustifiable, although Haman persuaded the king that the Jews were potential troublemakers who should be put out of the way.

This is the same argument used by Nazi Germany during 1939-1945, when five and a half million Jews perished in gas-chambers and concentration camps.

The only satisfactory explanation of the terrible sufferings of the "chosen people" throughout history is to be found in the constant opposition of Satan to God. The Messiah was to come through the seed of Abraham, and it was Satan's aim to make His coming impossible by wiping out the nation.

Among other nations there have been many attempts to invade lands, subjugate people, even to make people slaves to the conqueror. The Napoleonic wars saw Britain and France in mortal combat for years. This was the great power struggle of the late 17th and early 18th centuries. But there was never any desire on either side to exterminate each other's peoples.

World War II saw terrible battles in Europe and the Pacific with great losses. More than 20 million died in Soviet Russia: Germans, Russians, Poles, Hungarians, Rumanians. Yet even in all this there was no attempt to exterminate peoples (except for the Jews in Germany). Subjugate them, maltreat them, drain them financially, reduce them to peasants, yes; completely destroy them, no!

Satan alone is behind all plans to exterminate the Jews. He would have succeeded in Egypt if God had not intervened.

Let us always remember that they who seek to destroy the Jews find themselves fighting God, and there is no future in such a battle. It is like banging your head against a brick wall: the only beneficial result is when you stop.

9
Esther 4:1-17

Mordecai's Grief/Esther 4:1-6

It is in a crisis that character is revealed. Some men and women may appear strong and steadfast in days of pleasantness and ease, when the soft south wind of summer blows across their lives; but comes adversity and tragedy howling like the northern winter wind, and their strength fades and fails.

Mordecai now shows us the man that he really was. Strong enough to stand firm for all he believed, yet tender to the point where he could weep over the anticipated sufferings of his countrymen.

His own life was one thing; yet now, because of his refusal to bow to Haman, every Jewish man, woman, boy and girl was to die. Not because of crimes committed; not because of rebellion against the monarchy: simply because they were Mordecai's people and Haman's hatred was directed against him.

Mordecai's outward demonstration of sorrow shows how deeply he agonized for his people. Sackcloth and ashes were the accepted symbols of mourning as Mordecai went throughout the city bewailing the fate of his people. He even went right up to the king's gate, where he probably hoped that someone from the court might see him. This worked, for the news was quickly brought to Esther of Mordecai's strange behavior. He was certainly the object of court chatter!

Verse 2 gives us a brief insight into the sacredness of the king's person. No one in mourning might intrude within the dwelling place of the great king; no sorrow was to come before the brightness of his face.

Deioces, founder of the Median monarchy, was the first to surround the person of the king with an almost sacred privacy. He was to be seen by no one; none were to enter into his presence; all things were to be done through messengers. The Persians adopted this with one exception: the appointing of seven chamberlains who could act as counselors and advisors. All of this shows up later when Mordecai makes his request to Esther.

Esther of course, was utterly bewildered by the action of Mordecai. She had no knowledge yet of the edict from Haman, and could only think he must be in personal trouble such as loss of money or property. So she tried to help in these areas by sending fresh clothing by the hand of her servant Hatach, with instructions to find out exactly what had taken place to cause Mordecai such deep sorrow.

Verse 3 describes for us the devastating effect the news of the edict had as it reached each province, and as the residents learned how long they had to live.

Those in Shushan, who heard it first, had 12 months to "sweat it out." By the time some of the farthest provinces heard the word, the time would be reduced to weeks. December 13 (using our calendar) was to be D day for the Jews: Death, Destruction, Devastation and Desolation.

Mordecai's Appeal to Esther/
Esther 4:7-17

Mordecai told Hatach of the edict and gave him a copy for Esther so that she could read it for herself. Then he demanded that she go in to the king and plead with him for the release of her people from their promised destruction.

Esther's reply was prompt and very clear. "What you are asking may be desirable but it is totally impossible. Even the least important inhabitant of the kingdom knows that no one can enter the king's presence unless called by the king, and I have not been called for a month. To go without such a call is certain death, unless he holds out the golden sceptre." She could easily have added, "How could I risk my young life on the whim of a man whose appreciation of human life is almost negligible?"

Eventually the reply of Esther was conveyed to Mordecai. His reply has become a classic in Holy Scripture and throughout history. "Think not with thyself that thou shalt escape in the king's house, more than all the Jews. For if thou altogether holdest thy peace at this time, then shall there enlargement and deliverance arise to the Jews from another place; but thou and thy father's house shall be destroyed: and who knoweth whether thou art come to the kingdom for such a time as this?" (v.v. 13,14).

This appeal is just about perfect! The right amount of pressure to produce the right kind of fear! "Esther, *you* are a Jewess, so remember December 13 is your D day too. Being queen cannot save you, for as you know, the king is always subject to his own laws."

The right amount of faith at the right time! "Enlargement and deliverance will come. If *you* fail, *God* cannot. But Esther, you will go down in history as the worst kind of failure, unwilling to risk your life to save your people."

Finally the great appeal to a new look at the situation in the light of God's sovereignty in her own life. "Think back Esther, when you came to me as a helpless orphaned refugee, and where you are today. Can't you see something of God's guidance and blessing? A Jewish queen on a Persian throne! Esther, surely you can see His hand? Who knows whether it is for this very reason you are where you are right now?"

Such reasoning is necessary for each of us. Why am I where I am? Is it my choosing or His? Remember; when you are in the place of His choosing, only then can He use you as His chosen instrument to bless His people.

The whole of church history has become a testimony to what Mordecai said that day. His words certainly moved Esther into quick and powerful action. A certain amount of time was available— December 13 was months away—so she asked for three days of fasting, which would surely be accompanied by prayer. Mordecai would gather the Jews on the outside and Esther would fast with her maids in the palace. Then Esther would act, literally taking her life in her hands, with these brave words: "If I perish, I perish."

Crisis has revealed the strong character. Now we are to see how brightly Esther's inner nature shines in the hour of decision. "If I perish, I perish" represents the high point of her dedication. She had nothing greater to offer than her life. Let's get this in perspective. Mordecai could be twenty to thirty years older than Esther. He had already lived much of his life, but she was young and beautiful, and there was so much for her yet to see and do.

It is this deliberate act of being willing to die which makes such a decision precious. To take a calculated risk in wartime is one thing, knowing that more survive than die in our modern battles. But to take your life in your hands knowing the odds against coming out alive are all against you is courage of the highest quality, far beyond the call of duty.

10
Esther 5:1-14; 6:1-14

**Esther's Appearance Before the King/
Esther 5:1-8**

The three days of fasting and prayer were over and
the time for action drew near. There is a good lesson
here for all of us in respect to prayer, faith and personal responsibility. Esther and Mordecai were fully
aware that only God could lay siege to the heart of
the monarch. Nevertheless, since the issue is the appearance of Esther before him unrequested, she must
look her loveliest. It was her great beauty that won
his heart in the first place, and now she adorned
herself in the royal apparel to go before the king as
his queen.

Let us remember some of the things we ask God
to do for us He expects us to do for ourselves. Grace,
strength, power He will give us, but so often we have

to *do*; here is Esther doing all she can, but trusting God to work the miracle with the king.

The moment of decision came as she stood in the court. The king sees her. Whatever surprise or even shock he may have felt at her unexpected presence, he was utterly consumed by her beauty. In the language of love, he extended to her the royal sceptre, bidding her enter and state the reason for her coming.

So deeply did the king love Esther that before she could ask anything specific, he offered her anything she wanted, even to half the kindgom. These are extravagant words which need to be understood in the language of the day; but they certainly meant she could have anything in reason. At a later day, Salome the dancer, offered the same choice by King Herod, chose the head of John the Baptist. The request was granted; and similarly there is no doubt that Esther could have had Haman removed. But that would never save her people, so she played for a little more time by inviting the king and Haman to a banquet later that day. Her request was granted immediately.

Later, at the banquet, the king asked Esther to state her request so that he may grant it to her. Again she delayed her answer, asking that just Haman and the king attend a special banquet the next day.

Arrangements were made and the preparation would begin for the great tomorrow.

Haman's Great Day/Esther 5:9-14

This was a day for Haman to remember! The Jews would be wiped out on December 13—the $20 million would produce a harvest of treasures from the spoiling of the Jews before their execution! He had been promoted to the highest place open to a man in Persia next to the monarch—King in everything but name! He was recognized as such in the court. Outside, amid the thronging population, everywhere people bowed to him in reverence. This was meat and drink to him. Now the queen herself wanted him for a banquet which only the king and he were to attend. Could it be that even the queen was impressed with his person? Maybe she had even fallen for him!

Pride always goes before a fall, but Haman was on cloud nine as he left the royal apartments. There was only one fly in the ointment—Mordecai the Jew, who refused to bow when Haman passed. However, it must not spoil a wonderful day, so "he refrained himself."

Can you imagine a man like Haman, almost exploding with excitement, then trying to put on a smile for the adoring crowds, and attempting to ignore the straight-backed, erect figure of Mordecai?

Eventually Haman arrived home, and all the restraint could go. He burbled out his great and glorious news—advancement, promotion, and now the unique invitation to Esther's banquet. Yet all of this brings no joy while Mordecai refused to bow!

It is amazing how a man can have everything in life as Haman did, and yet one person can take away all the enjoyment. Haman's pride was hurt; to think that anyone dared withstand his command! Of course December 13 would take care of Mordecai, but there were months of insubordination still ahead.

Behind every good man or every man that has made good there is generally some woman who has had a great part in making him what he now is—often a mother, a wife, or a sister. Equally, history often shows that a wicked man is made worse by a wicked wife. Ahab would be a fine example of this. Bad as he was, the evil force in Israel was Jezebel; she left her name to posterity as an example of wickedness.

Haman had such a wife in the person of Zeresh. Her reasoning was clear, her method simple. "You are the great and mighty Haman, do you mean to tell me you are going to be upset by one miserable Jew? Why wait until December 13? You are the power in the land, so get a gallows and have Mordecai strung up by sunset tomorrow."

"Why didn't I think of it," thought Haman. "A great idea! I'll get the carpenters to work. Oh, what a day tomorrow will be! The banquet with Esther and the king, and Mordecai will be out of the way forever."

Haman went to bed a self-satisfied man. Esther went to bed planning her strategy to save her people. Mordecai went to bed wondering how Esther had fared in the palace. And the king went to bed anticipating yet another banquet! Not *all* of them would sleep, for God was beginning to move in to deliver His people!

The King's Sleeplessness/Esther 6:1-3

Do you think God has a sense of humor? I hope you do, for now we are going to see God demonstrate His sovereignty in such a way as to produce one of the best laughs of all time, and yet at the same time solemnly intervene to save His people.

Haman had gone to bed with a song in his heart ("I'm sitting on top of the world" would have suited his mood!) and with glowing anticipation of a wonderful tomorrow. He probably slept like a child.

But there was one man who could not sleep—the king! Imagine such a strange thing, a king who cannot sleep. With silken sheets and the best of beds, surely sleep would be automatic. Maybe it was generally so, but not that night. No amount of Sominex or aspirin would help him; no soft music; nothing could induce sleep because God wanted him awake.

Learn a lesson now if you do not know it already. God can reach any man at any time, no matter who he is, what he is, where he is or what he is doing. This is another area of the sovereignty of God.

The king, unable to sleep, decided to read. He asked for the equivalent of our newspapers or magazines; the chronicles of the recent happenings in the court. His servants obeyed his wishes and began to read the news to him. Suddenly they reached the place telling of the time when Mordecai exposed the plot to assassinate the king. (See Esther 2:21-23.)

The king immediately asked what kind of reward had been given to this Mordecai who had saved the king's life; but a diligent search found no reward had been made. The monarch was astounded and shocked that no honor had been paid to his deliverer. He asked who was in the court that morning. He wanted one of his counselors to advise him about an appropriate reward for Mordecai.

The Pride and Fall of Haman/Esther 6:4-14

Now the fun starts. Haman had arrived especially early for what he thought was to be his big day. He wanted to inform the king that Mordecai would be hanged that day. Did ever a dawn break more propitiously for Haman than this one? If he had a song in his heart it surely would carry the sentiment of Rodgers and Hammerstein's, "Oh, what a beautiful morning, Oh, what a beautiful day ... everything's going my way." But as often stated— pride cometh before a fall!

An old saying that never loses its truth is this, "The mills of God grind slowly, but they grind exceeding small." You will never see this saying fulfilled more effectively than in this incident.

It is so interesting, and so funny! The king wondered what Haman wanted; Haman wondered what the king wanted. Neither knew the other was thinking about Mordecai. Haman was there for Mordecai's execution order; the king was there to honor Mordecai for saving his life; and Mordecai was totally unaware of the situation!

Haman greeted the king cordially and was asked by the monarch, "What shall be done to the man whom the king delights to honor?"

Pride ... pride ... pride always precedes a fall. Haman thought, "Who could the king want to honor more than me?" so he immediately revealed the state of his own mind as he said, "Let him be 'king for a day.' Let him wear the king's clothes and ride the king's horse. Proclaim a holiday, let him have a princely escort and the most noble man of all to announce to the people, 'This is the man whom the king delights to honor'" (vv. 7-9).

If the king had had his wits about him he would have spotted at once that Haman was a potential threat to the throne. "King for a day" could so easily become king every day.

At this point Haman could feel the horse under him, the royal raiment on him and the cheering crowds greeting him. But then came the greatest shock and the beginning of his downfall.

"Excellent, excellent," says the king. "One of your very best ideas, Haman; do exactly as you say to Mordecai the Jew; do everything you proposed." Can you imagine the utter mortification of Haman? He could not believe his ears! Mordecai the Jew, for whom his men were preparing a gallows! And do you still ask if God has a sense of humor?

Haman had to face the reality of the king's order. The horse was made ready, Mordecai mounted in glory and Haman started his march through the city calling on the inhabitants to welcome the man the king was honoring. This day which began so beautifully had taken a terrible turn for Haman, but his embarrassment now is only the prelude to his final overthrow and the deliverance of the Jews.

Before proceeding further, let us note that God has just two people to work with to save His people. Esther, the unknown orphan, He had placed on the throne of Persia; now He was moving to get Mordecai into a situation where he could influence the monarch and ultimately change the edict for the massacre of the Jews.

Shamed and humbled, Haman returned home in a state of mourning and shared his sorrow with his wife Zeresh and his advisors. Their reply is given in verse 13. Their statement is amazing for its truth and for the wisdom of those who made it. It indicates no fear of Mordecai as an individual, but of the race to which he belongs, the very race Haman is out to destroy.

These are indeed historic words. Egypt disappeared as a world power before the Jews; Assyria, Chaldea soon followed; and in our present age, the downfall of Nazi Germany was certain once she started murdering Jews. Let all of us remember and never forget that he who would destroy the Jews must destroy God first. God said it, meant it and has done it: "I will make of thee (Abraham) a great nation . . . and in thee shall all the families of the earth be blessed" (Gen. 12:2,3). "For all the land (Canaan) which thou seest, to thee (Abraham) will I give it, and to thy seed (Isaac) for ever" (Gen. 13:15). God cannot be broken; His promises cannot fail. The words of Haman's advisors represent sound and solid fact. They were saying, "If Mordecai really is a Jew, then leave him alone right now. You are already a loser today, so get out before you are brought to complete destruction."

Time, however was running out. The chamberlains were there to escort Haman to Esther's banquet, and all the joy he had in anticipating this event must have turned to dread as he wondered what fresh tragedy could befall him.

11

Esther 7:1-10; 8:1-17

Esther's Great Intercession/Esther 7:1-10

Our story now swings back to the courageous queen who had to face the great ordeal of revealing her race to the king, pleading for her people, and confronting Haman with his evil plan. Keep in mind the position of women these days. They had no personal rights, and for a woman to stand up to any man was unheard of (remember what happened to Vashti in chapters 1 and 2). Esther was showing tremendous courage at this time.

As the banquet progressed, the king encouraged Esther to make her request with the customary assurance, "It shall be granted unto half the kingdom."

Esther had such a comfortable life, why should she get involved? Because her countrymen were in great danger, and love of God means love of people and love of the land which gave her birth. Personally she was doing well, but her people would be wiped out on December 13 unless the edict was changed. This was the burden of her heart as she made her supplication to the king.

She began with herself because she knew the king loved her with whatever love he had: "Let my life be given me . . . and my people at my request: For we are sold, I and my people, to be destroyed, to be slain, and to perish. But if we had been sold for bondmen and bondwomen, I had held my tongue, although the enemy could not countervail the king's damage" (vv. 3,4). The last part of Esther's plan means, "although the money paid into the king's treasures by the enemy (Haman) would never compensate the king for the loss of so many of his subjects."

Let her plea be a lesson to us all. We need people today who can pray to God in such intercessions for their country, people who are identified with and involved in the life of the nation. Like Paul, in another day, who cried in his praying, "Brethren, my heart's desire (the burning passion of my heart), and prayer to God for Israel is, that they might be saved" (Rom. 10:1).

Esther was bold, her words were plain, her request was direct, her heart was open. She was not playing games, she was pleading for lives; and the simplicity and sincerity of her words reached the king's heart.

His response was immediate. "Who would even dare to threaten the life of my lovely queen and her people?" Esther, with great courage, stated, "The adversary and enemy is this wicked Haman."

The king was filled with wrath, and Haman was in great fear. As the king walked through the gardens in an attempt to pacify himself, Haman decided to plead for his life, casting himself on the mercy of Esther. He could see his future in the service of the king had gone; his only concern was to save his skin.

Once things go wrong, they really move, and nothing was going right for Haman. Esther was reclining on her bed, and Haman was beside her, begging for his life, when the king returned. The ruler took one look, and jumped to the wrong conclusion. Haman was finished. In all fairness to Haman, the last thought in his mind was to assault Esther, but how the tables had turned on this enemy of God's people.

"The mills of God" were surely grinding, and there was one more turn before they ceased. The king's anger knew no control; Haman must die. One of the king's chamberlains was on hand to say, "As a matter of fact, sire, there is this new set of gallows which Haman has had erected for Mordecai. It would be a shame not to use it." The king's decision was quick and final: "Hang him on it." And so passes into history that which has a lesson for all of us. Beware that the plans you have to harm and damage someone are not turned about in similar fashion by God, bringing destruction upon your own head.

The Elevation of Mordecai/Esther 8:1-8

"Who knows whether thou art come to the kingdom for such a time as this" had been Mordecai's word to Esther in her darkest hour. Now, with Haman dead, a new dawn was breaking and she must have felt that her last request to save her people would be granted by the king.

She took Mordecai to the king, who now saw the man who had saved his life. But the gratitude he felt for this must have been secondary to the emotions that gripped him when Esther revealed who Mordecai was to her and all he had done for her. Surely with admiration and affection the king looked at Mordecai, the one who was "father and mother" to his beautiful Esther, who had raised her through childhood and had helped to shape the inner beauty of her lovely nature.

All of Haman's property had been given to Esther; and in the ceremony of ring-giving, Mordecai was appointed controller over Haman's house. Do you still wonder if God has a sense of humor?

Now God had His two people in position. He could move to deliver His nation. Esther was granted an audience by the king; she asked outright for the repeal of Haman's edict and the substitution of a new law giving to the Jews the rights and privileges they formerly enjoyed as the king's subjects.

Worthy of special note is the intensity of the appeal from Esther's heart, contained in verse 6. "For how can I endure to see the evil that shall come unto my people? or how can I endure to see the destruction of my kindred?" (A question for us all: How much can we endure to see in the life of our country today? Have we any burden for our people and our nation?)

Deliverance of the Jews/Esther 8:9-17

The appeal reached the king's heart, but he could not simply repeal the former edict. No one, not even the king himself, had the power to reverse the laws of the Medes and Persians. (Compare the similar problem of Darius the Mede in Daniel 6.) However, the king could issue a new law, which would modify

83

the effects of the first one, and would be just as binding. Ahasuerus gave Mordecai the job of writing the new edict.

Once written, the new edict had to be delivered throughout the empire. Verses 10-12 give us the situation in a nutshell. The old message would be well on its way to the farthest territories belonging to Persia. The new law had to be copied in all the various languages, then the riders (the original pony express) would have to ride faster to make sure everyone had the word before D day, December 13.

There would be Jew-haters in every place, so the new law made provision for the Jews to defend themselves against the attack. Still working on our calendar, it would be the end of March when Mordecai took over, so time was a big factor; the edict to destroy all Jews on December 13 would be carried out if the new law did not arrive in time.

Shushan, being the capital, had been the first to receive the disastrous news (chapter 3:15): now it was the first to hear the good! Contrast the former sackcloth and ashes of Mordecai (4:1,2) with his manner and bearing now. He went forth a commanding figure, clothed in royal apparel of blue and white, with a crown of gold and outer garments of fine linen and purple. He was regal to the last degree!

Rejoicing was the order of the day! God expects His people to rejoice at the right time, even as He expects them to sorrow when the time requires it. Sorrow they had had, but the dread of the coming December 13 was over now. It was like the prisoner in the condemned cell receiving a free pardon just prior to his execution.

The Jews had light, gladness, joy and honor. As

the new law reached each city and town, the place was taken over by rejoicing days. Feasting and gladness took over and the Jews had a good day! It was liberation day for thousands and thousands, and thousands more would join in as the news reached them. It recalls the end of World War II in Europe, when the victorious armies of the Allies opened up the P.O.W. camps in their great sweep across Germany.

The closing section of verse 17 is very interesting! "And many of the people of the land became Jews; for the fear of the Jews fell upon them." This is one of the earliest illustrations of the well-worn statement, "If you can't beat them, join them!" Although they could not be Jews by birth, they could embrace the Jewish faith and become proselytes. The history of the Jews is simple: when they are obedient and God is blessing them they become the envy of all; but when they are disobedient and God hides His face from them, they suffer so much at the hands of others that no one desires to be associated with them.

12
Esther 9:1-32; 10:1-3

**The Destruction of the Enemies of the Jews/
Esther 9:1-19**

There is a natural abhorrence of vengeance in
every Christian heart. We seek to manifest the for-
giveness our Lord taught and exemplified in His own
life, and we should never seek vengeance on those
who seek our hurt. But we must never confuse judicial action with personal action. Look for instance at
the death penalty (whether you agree or disagree
with it does not affect the illustration). When the
judge hears the "guilty" verdict from the jury he
pronounces the death sentence, but he has not killed
the accused. Nor has the executioner killed the condemned even though he has pulled the lever. An
execution is a judicial, not a personal, matter.

December 13 dawned—D day for the Jews until
the new law came. Thanks to that new law, they were

ready to defend themselves against all comers. Note the operative and key word is *defend*. They were not to carry out a revenge murder program against their former enemies.

Many of the Persian army officers on duty in each land allied themselves with the Jews for "the fear of [the Jews] fell upon all people." The Persians could not pinpoint where the miracles on behalf of the Jews came from, but they had to recognize the reality of some unknown, yet effective, power working mightily in their favor.

Let's get a proper appreciation of the position. The Jewish population in Persia was in the area of two and a half to three million, including children. The population of the Persian empire was 73 million. There is no way the three million could ever constitute any kind of threat to the existence of the other 70 million. The fear experience was God-given.

People are bound to be killed in such circumstances, with tempers aflame and the irresponsible elements to be found in every community. There was no indiscriminate slaughter of the masses, but many died on this day of reckoning. About 75,000 people were killed by the Jews. However, it is only fair to point out that this is from a population of 73 million, and also to recall that this was the appointed day for the massacre of three million Jews.

Esther's request for Haman's sons to be hanged seems out of line with her general character, but let us remember that this was no personal vengeance she sought. Rather, it was done to deepen the impression made upon all the people by the just retribution which befell those responsible for the terrible plot to massacre God's people.

Law and order came from God, and the breaking of the law always brings punishment and suffering. Men may get away with their evil for years, but eventually the truth will out and suffering and dishonor will come to the culprit, with shame to his family and friends.

December 13 was the day the Jews had feared—now it was to be a day to recall with great thankfulness and joy. Their mourning turned to dancing. Celebration was the order of every Jewish community. God had done it again! He had not cast off His people! He had intervened and turned certain defeat into glorious victory.

They sent gifts to each other, and especially to the poor. The overflowing heart always finds a way to express itself in caring for the less fortunate.

Now as our story is coming to its conclusion, we do well to think yet again of the greatness of our majestic God who maneuvered His two servants to the highest places in Persia, thus insuring the safety and welfare of His people, and, incidentally, the prosperity of the Persian empire.

How we need to relearn the truth, "Blessed is the nation whose God is the Lord" (Ps. 33:12). God's people, walking in obedience to His revealed will, can be a tremendous potential for good in their land. God always blesses righteousness.

The Festival of Purim/Esther 9:20-32

Mordecai now sets out to establish December 13 as the day of deliverance, and to institute a continuing memorial through all generations. It is to be called *Pur*—meaning *the lot* (Esther 9:24)—but because of remote territory and time changes, it became two days instead of one. Thus both days are to be kept and it will be known as the feast of *Purim* (*Purim* being the plural form of *Pur*).

Esther sends the directive to every part of the Empire, calling upon Jews to set apart these two days in which to give thanks and praise to God for His wonderful deliverance. There would be days of rejoicing, feasting and fellowship. Each generation would be responsible to tell the story to the one following.

How marvelously this was carried out is seen in our own time, some 2500 years later, when orthodox Jews worldwide keep the Feast of Purim. This is another instance of the absolute truth of the Bible.

The Closing Picture of Mordecai/ Esther 10:1-3

Now clearly established at the king's right hand, Mordecai became responsible for the king's revenue. Xerxes (Ahasuerus) was a forerunner of I.R.S. in that he introduced a universal tax; Mordecai saw that it was collected and not squandered.

The events of this period are covered by Persian historians, who indicate that Persia grew strong and prosperous under the capable administration of Mordecai. He was honored among his own people. He was accepted in his position by the multitude of his brethren. He constantly sought their prosperity, together with policies to establish peace for succeeding generations of his people.

God never makes a mistake, and yet He will take a man from total obscurity and set him in the place of highest importance. Only God knew that Mordecai had the ability to run a nation, and He saw to it that the opportunity came for Mordecai to use his latent gifts.

Mordecai was not a nincompoop nor the village idiot. He had what it took, but only God could provide the means for him to be what he could be. Only God knows your capabilities; that is why it is vital that your life is totally surrendered to Him. You will never become what you should be unless the Lord is in absolute control of your life.

Mordecai found his true gift and his true glory in serving his people as prime minister of Persia. He never attempted to feather his own nest, but used his great power for the benefit and blessing of all.

13
Esther 1-10

The Value and Meaning
of the Book of Esther Today

The outstanding lesson to be learned from the book is the sovereignty of God. While this could be said of every book in the Bible, it is demonstrated more clearly here than anywhere. By sovereignty is meant that *God is on the throne.* All nations, people and lands are under His control. He controls the universe and all the wonderful forces of nature. As we sing so heartily, "He's got the whole world in His hand."

This means that present world happenings may upset us but they never disturb Him. Financial problems may overwhelm us, but they never take Him by surprise. God is never taken unaware by the events of history, for He makes history. He knows the end from the beginning and never has to wait and see how things turn out. He does not have to wait for speeches by national leaders to know their policy or the direction their country will take.

God's ability to work with the absolute minimum to do the absolute maximum is clearly demonstrated in Esther. There were 73 million Persians, and three million Jews; and God changed the whole course of history with just two people! This should be a source of tremendous encouragement to every Christian believer, and the essence of all motivation in Christian service. How marvelous to know you are always on the winning side! All of us suffer personal defeats at the hand of Satan, yet we are on the victory side and will come out triumphant because our *God is on the throne.*

The second lesson to profit us is this: God takes years to prepare His servants for what may prove to be a short but vital period for service.

Let us illustrate this from the life of the Lord Jesus first. He had thirty years of sinless living in an almost unknown area of the world—the Roman-occupied garrison town of Nazareth. He was raised in comparative obscurity and poverty, content to be known as the village carpenter. Then He had three years of public ministry—preaching, teaching and healing—before dying on Calvary. Finally, He rose again, triumphant over sin, death, the grave, hell and Satan. Note His words: "The hour is come . . . what shall I say? Father, save me from this hour; but for this cause came I unto this hour" (John 12:23,27). This does not mean the rest of the time did not count. Every hour counted, but Christ never lost sight of the real purpose of His coming.

God had watched over Esther through the loss of her family and her trip to Persia. He still watched over her under the guardianship of Mordecai. Mordecai points out this second lesson for us in his reminder to Esther that she may have been brought to the kingdom for such a time as this.

It is not for us to choose our path, nor to estimate our usefulness in any given situation. God never wastes anything, and certainly not the lives of His servants. We all have an important part to play in the Kingdom of God, but He alone has the right to designate our service and the geographical location where we exercise it. Learn to obey the first time! We never know what is our "greatest" hour; only God knows that. But let us remember some words of Winston Churchill during the Battle of Britain in 1941. "We have the honor to stand alone! Let us so conduct ourselves in these days of crisis that when future historians write the story of our people they will say, 'This was their finest hour.' "

Let us so live that every day will count for God.

The third lesson from Esther is that God generally gets His people into position before He needs them. God doesn't rush in at the last minute to try to straighten out previous mistakes. God never makes a mistake and never gets into a panic. God engineers the circumstances just as He requires to accomplish His perfect will and purpose.

Esther was on the throne in time to intercede; Mordecai overheard the plan to assassinate the king; the matter was recorded in the court chronicles and promptly forgotten until the night the king could not sleep. This book teaches the wonderful ability of God to handle the most difficult situations and turn them to His glory. After all, what man or group of men can match God in wisdom?

The fourth message to us is the wonderful time-keeping of our timeless God! Time—hours, days, weeks, years—we measure by the sun. God has no such limitation, yet He can work within the framework of humanity and always be there to rescue His people "in the nick of time." This was so powerfully demonstrated when Haman chose D day for the Jews. God said something like, "I will remember that date and prepare something Haman will never forget."

What a comfort to know our God is not only the Master Designer but also the Master of detail. How thrilling to know that the God of Esther and Mordecai is our God too!

How wonderful to know that the One we read about in Scripture is the One we now worship; the God and Father of our Lord Jesus Christ who loves us with an everlasting love and is the same yesterday, today and forever.

Let us give all we have and are to serve Him joyfully until we see Him face to face in eternal glory.